ONE**DUCK**

FLIGHTS

by John O'Donovan

Flights was first performed on 15th January 2020 at glór, Ennis.

FLIGHTS

by John O'Donovan

Cast

BARRY	Colin Campbell
CUSACK	Conor Madden
PA	Rhys Dunlop

Creative Team

Director	Thomas Martin
Set and Costume	Naomi Faughnan
Lighting	Zia Bergin-Holly
Sound and Composition	Peter Power
Movement	Sue Mythen
Production Manager	Eoin Kilkenny
Deputy Stage Manager	Emily Danby
Hair and Make-up Consultant	Val Sherlock
Producer and Stage Manager	Alan Mahon

A One Duck production funded by the Arts Council of Ireland.

CAST

COLIN CAMPBELL | BARRY

Colin is a graduate of The Lir Academy.

His theatre credits include *The Comedy of Errors*, *Pericles*, *Twelfth Night* (Shakespeare's Globe/world tour); *Cuckoo* (Soho Theatre); *Scotties* (Theatre Gu Leòr, Glasgow); *Disco Pigs* (Tara Finney Productions, Irish Rep Theatre NY); *Dublin by Lamplight*, *Through a Glass Darkly* (The Corn Exchange); *East of Berlin* (Project Arts Centre).

CONOR MADDEN | CUSACK

Conor is a graduate of the Trinity College Dublin BA in Acting Studies. Recent theatre credits include *Bread Not Profits* for Gúna Nua Theatre Company and *The Rehearsal: Playing the Dane* for Pan Pan Theatre Company at the Dublin Theatre Festival which went on to tour to the US, Australia, New Zealand and Korea and most recently appeared in the Abbey Theatre. On screen, Conor has appeared in *Love/Hate* written by Stuart Carolan and directed by David Caffrey, *RAW* and *The Clinic* (RTÉ) and as Eric Trygvasson in *Vikings* (History Channel/MGA).

RHYS DUNLOP | PA

Rhys is a graduate of The Lir Academy. For One Duck, he wrote and performed *Lad* with Alan Mahon.

After graduating from The Lir in 2014 Rhys went straight into playing the lead role in *Punk Rock* by Simon Stephens for which he was nominated for an Irish Times Theatre Award for Best Actor. Recent acting credits include *Dead Still* and *Resistance* (RTÉ); *Come Home, The Truth Commissioner* and *Doctors* (BBC); *Surrogate* (Blackpills); *L'Ascension* (Mars Intl Film); *The Secret* (ITV); *Madame Geneva* (Lyric Theatre, Belfast); *Sacrifice at Easter* (Corcadorca); *Shibboleth* (Abbey Theatre); *A Skull in Connemara* (Nottingham Playhouse) and *Shoot The Crow* (Primecut Productions).

CREATIVE TEAM

JOHN O'DONOVAN | WRITER
John is a writer from Clarecastle, Co. Clare. This is his third collaboration with One Duck. His plays include *If We Got Some More Cocaine I Could Show You How I Love You* (published by Methuen Drama), *Hy Brasil*, *Flights* and *Sink* (published by Nick Hern Books). A former member of the Royal Court Young Writers Programme, Old Vic 12 and BBC Drama Room, he was awarded the 2017 IARA Award for Best Playwright and the 2018 Stewart Parker Trust/BBC Northern Ireland Radio Drama Award. He has had stories, plays and articles published in the *Irish Times, Verbal Arts Magazine, Crannóg* and *Bare Fiction*.

THOMAS MARTIN | DIRECTOR
Thomas is a freelance theatre director. For One Duck, he has directed *Lad*, *Sink* and *If We Got Some More Cocaine I Could Show You How I Love You*.

His production of Margaret Perry's *Collapsible* will play London's Bush Theatre in February 2020, after its award-winning runs at the Edinburgh Fringe and the Abbey Theatre, as part of Dublin Fringe.

Other directing credits include *Ross & Rachel* (Edinburgh Fringe; Brits Off-Broadway/two UK tours); *Siren* (Edinburgh Fringe; VAULT 2018); *Bromley, Bedlam, Bethlehem* (Old Red Lion) and *Followers* (Southwark Playhouse). Work with young people and non-professionals has included: *Sing Before You Speak Again* (Young Vic Taking Part); *Talk Me Down* (Cambridge Junction Young Company) and *Auto-Play* (Bush Theatre/White City Youth Theatre).

NAOMI FAUGHNAN | SET AND COSTUME
Naomi is a multi-disciplinary designer, maker, stylist and tutor working in theatre, film, TV and fashion. A graduate of The Lir Academy with an MFA in Stage Design and a Degree in Fashion Design, she is currently participating in the Rough Magic SEEDS programme as the Set and Costume Designer. Some of her credits include *Trad* (Livin Dred); *Minefield* by Clare Monnelly (Dublin Fringe); *We Can't Have Monkeys in the House* by Ciara Elizabeth Smith (Abbey Theatre); *INFINITY* by Eoghan Carrick and Nessa Matthews (Dublin Fringe) and *Murder of Crows* (Theatre Upstairs). She finds inspiration in the mundane and revels in its transformation.

ZIA BERGIN-HOLLY | LIGHTING
Zia won the 2017 Irish Times Theatre Award for Best Lighting Design for her design of Pan Pan Theatre's *The Importance of Nothing*.

Recent lighting designs include *Promises Promises* (Centrál Színház, Budapest); *Top Hat* (Silver Blue Entertainment); *Ignition 2019* (Frantic Assembly); *Cleft* (Rough Magic); *Bread Not Profits* (Gúna Nua); *Apologia* and *The Lion in Winter* (English Theatre Frankfurt); *Vespertilio* (VAULT Festival); *The Bystander* (Junk Ensemble); *Frankie and Johnny in the Clair de Lune* (Northern Stage); *Romeo and Juliet* (Ballet Ireland); *The Ladykillers* (The Lyric Theatre, Belfast) and *The Nest* (Lyric Theatre/ Young Vic Theatre). Set and lighting designs include *The Misfits* (Corn Exchange, Dublin) and *User Not Found* (Dante or Die).

PETER POWER | SOUND AND COMPOSITION
Peter is a composer, director and sound designer who works in theatre, events and film.

He holds a BSC in Biochemistry and an MA in Composition. His interests are in collaborative creation using music as non-linear narrative. He is Artistic Director of Sparsile Collective and Director of multi-genre audio duo Eat My Noise. Peter is the previous Artist-in-Residence in the National Sculpture Factory and the New Artist-in-Residence of the Cork Midsummer Festival. He received a Music Bursary in 2017 and a Project Award in 2018 from the Arts Council of Ireland. Recent work includes *The Same* by Enda Walsh, *In Clouds* by Sparsile Collective, and *ProdiJig* by Cork Opera House.

SUE MYTHEN | MOVEMENT
Sue is an award-winning movement director working in theatre, opera and film.

Work for One Duck includes *If We Got Some More Cocaine I Could Show You How I Love You* by John O'Donovan. Recent credits include *Asking for it* (Gaiety Theatre/Everyman Theatre/Birmingham Rep/Abbey Theatre); *Citysong* (Abbey Theatre/Soho Theatre); *The Lost O'Casey* (ANU); *On Raftery's Hill* (Abbey Theatre); *Crestfall* (Druid); *Private Peaceful* (Irish and US tours); *Radamisto* (NI Opera); *The White Devil* (Shakespeare's Globe) and *The Heiress* (The Gate).

Her work on screen includes *Northanger Abbey* (ITV); *History's Future* (CineArtNederland) and *Normal People* (BBC). Sue is Head of Movement at The Lir Academy, TCD.

EOIN KILKENNY | PRODUCTION MANAGER
Eoin is a freelance project and production manager. He has worked previously with Landmark Productions on *Once* (Dublin, Seoul), *Howie the Rookie* and *These Halcyon Days*. He has worked in venues and festivals across Ireland and the UK, including Edinburgh Fringe, the Abbey Theatre and the National Concert Hall. Eoin has toured with musicians and bands such as Gabby Young, CODES, Colm Wilkinson and the Irish Baroque Orchestra. Eoin is a product of UCD Dramsoc and holds an MA from the Royal Central School of Speech and Drama.

EMILY DANBY | DEPUTY STAGE MANAGER
Emily is a stage manger with over fifteen years' experience. She started her career at the Young Vic Theatre in London. She has also worked at the Gate Theatre and the Royal Court Theatre. Emily moved overseas for a time and worked with the New Zealand Opera and Auckland Theatre Company. She has recently moved to Ireland from Scotland where she worked as a producer for the theatre company Ludens Ensemble.

More recently Emily has been working in film and television and was a location assistant for the STV/BBC production of *Elizabeth is Missing*.

ALAN MAHON | PRODUCER
Alan is a graduate of The Lir Academy and Artistic Director of One Duck. He wrote and performed *Lad* with Rhys Dunlop.

Acting credits include *My Romantic History* (Verdant Productions); *Last Night in Soho* by Edgar Wright (Big Smoke Pictures); *Resistance* (RTÉ/Netflix); *Caterpillar* (Theatre503); *Alkaline* (Park Theatre); *If We Got Some More Cocaine I Could Show You How I Love You* (One Duck 2018/Old Red Lion 2016); *Brutal Cessation* (Edinburgh Fringe/Theatre503); *Hamlet* and *All's Well That Ends Well* (Tobacco Factory/UK tour); *King Lear* (Second Age); *The Windstealers* (Dublin Fringe); *The Waste Ground Party* (Abbey Theatre) and *Fair City* (RTÉ).

ONEDUCK

One Duck was founded in Dublin in 2016 with the aim of producing new plays that provoke and entertain.

Their body of work includes *Lad* by Alan Mahon and Rhys Dunlop and *Sink* by John O'Donovan (both at Dublin Fringe Festival, 2019); *If We Got Some More Cocaine I Could Show You How I Love You* by John O'Donovan (Project Arts Centre, glór, Mick Lally Theatre and VAULT Festival, 2018) and *The Poor Little Boy With No Arms* which was devised at The Lir Academy (Project Arts Centre and Irish tour, 2016).

Upcoming work at VAULT Festival 2020 includes a work-in-progress reading of new play *A Young Man Comes* by Alan Mahon on 5th February and our production of *Lad* by Alan Mahon and Rhys Dunlop from 4th to 8th March.

We would like to thank the Arts Council of Ireland; Allen Flynn and all the staff at the Old Ground Hotel; Sean Dennehy; Diana Whitehead and Fourth Wall PR; Martha Hegarty; Michelle Barnette; Ekaterina Solmatina; Fionn Walton; Paul Mescal; James Foley; Lara Beach; Daragh MacLachlan; Irish Theatre Institute; CoisCéim Dance Theatre; The Lir Academy; Orla Flanagan and everyone at glór; Cian O'Brien and everyone at Project Arts Centre; Marie McCarthy and everyone at Omnibus Theatre and, in particular, Dermot and Rachel McMahon for all their support with this production of *Flights*.

FLIGHTS

Author's Note

Flights is a play that's very close to my heart. I've been writing it on and off for about five years now, using characters that are kind of like grown-up versions of characters I wrote about in my first ever full-length play. Like *Sink*, it is set very specifically in the here and now (the here being the west of Ireland) while at the same time being about generational memory and the inescapability of histories – both personal and public.

Initially *Flights* was not much more than a fairly funny short play about someone throwing his own going-away party (that almost no one shows up to); but while I was sketching out that early draft, I got some bad news that a guy from back home had died by suicide.

A few of us living over in England got together once we heard the news – we weren't going home for the funeral so we went to a pub in London instead, aiming to share stories we had of him, and all the other people we'd known who've died prematurely over the years since school, whether through suicide, car accidents, drink or terminal illnesses.

It seemed like a lot – a dozen maybe? – definitely too many. But it also seemed kind of old hat, like we'd been here before. We already knew what to do: gather, tell stories, find out who to contact, ask if they wanted flowers or a donation, then get in touch with whoever we thought might need to be gotten in touch with and make sure again that we were all alright.

I've had a lot of conversations like that over the years. A lot of nights out on the beer in remembrance. Getting rounds in and sharing stories. Starting sombre, ending wild. Making sure to recall the funny stuff as well as the tragic bits. The anger and the pure silliness.

It becomes habitual, ritualistic. Something we remember when the anniversaries roll around. Something to keep in mind whenever we get the unwelcome phone call with the news.

That was the early impulse of *Flights* – a kind of tribute not just to all the friends who have died, but also to the friends that have gathered in their wake, who look out for each other, look after each other and remember to get in touch when the bad news spreads.

But the more I wrote, the more I realised that the story was not just about personal tragedy, but was also about the economic context in which these tragedies take place. As much as Barry, Cusack and Pa's teenage lives were stalled by Liam's death, they were equally paralysed in adulthood by the global recession; they made cautious choices, enforced by a lack of opportunities in front of them. And instinctively they learned that their lives were only useful insofar as they were put to work.

This is a punishing and limiting way to live, to be victims of an economy you are obliged to serve. Your creativity, your expression, even your physicality means nothing unless it's being used to earn and spend money. This ideology produces such a reckless attitude to body and mind, it is no wonder people turn in on themselves, heedless of their safety and capacity, assaulting their physical and mental health while struggling to imagine another way to live.

There's this patronising, anachronistic idea about men that they don't know what they're feeling – that if they just expressed themselves they wouldn't be so fucked up. But some of the things they feel – rage, weakness, fatigue, apathy – aren't the kinds of things that people want to hear about. It's all well and good telling fellas they need to talk, but when there's no one – trained or otherwise – prepared to listen, many will know it's easier to keep their mouths shut.

And these feelings are not peculiar: rage, weakness, fatigue and apathy are sensible responses to living under austerity capitalism.

So I don't think it's a crisis of masculinity alone; more that there's a crisis in health services, in housing, in employment and work–life balance – in other words, the same crises that have been devastating Ireland for more than a decade. Young men, like all young people, have been part of a generation disproportionately punished by austerity economics; the idea that their problems would disappear if they weren't too proud or macho to talk their way out of it is at best naive, and at worst an invidious piece of victim blaming that ignores economic causality and favours individual recrimination over systemic improvement.

To me, *Flights* is not a play about men not being able to articulate themselves; it's not filled with brooding, unsaid feelings. Silence is not their problem; if anything they have too many words. It's not the inability to speak, but the fact that they are speaking to a world that has no interest in listening that's troubling them. It's not unsayable truths but unavoidable facts that finally do for them: that not seeing a place for themselves in their country, or in the world, it should come as no surprise that they might want to take themselves out of it.

Flights starts and ends as an act of remembrance: three fellas come together in a world that's changing around them; old before their time, they're fading out of their own lives. Consumed with the history of their grief – and bereft of their own potential – they are more adept at remembering the past than they are at seeing clearly what's happening to them now.

If I could wish anything for them, it is that as much as they would never forget their friend and the promise they once shared, I hope they never forgive the economics that has left them behind, stewing, with their best days far behind them, lying stalled and stagnating, finished before they ever got started.

John O'Donovan,
January 2020

Acknowledgements

With thanks to Ailbhe Hogan, Michael Dee, Kieran Gough, Séamus Hughes, Cillian Roche, Kristina Izidora Sučić, Paul Mescal, Fionn Walton, Aaron Monaghan, Stewart Pringle, Clive Judd, Brad Birch, Jessica Stewart, Annabelle Comyn, Deirdre O'Halloran, Orla Flanagan and all at glór, Cian O'Brien and all at Project Arts Centre, Marie McCarthy and all at Omnibus Theatre, Matt Applewhite and all at NHB, Nick Quinn and all at The Agency, Marty Rea and all at Druid, Theatre503, the Irish Theatre Institute, the King's Head Theatre and The Lir Academy.

Special thanks to Thomas Martin for his help in breathing life into every draft of the play, and to Alan Mahon for resuscitating it when it looked like it was beyond hope.

John O'Donovan

'Pity me' I cried out to him,
'Whether it's a ghost you are or a man.'

Dante Alighieri, Inferno

We all partied.

Brian Lenihan TD, Minister for Finance,
November 2010

Characters

BARRY
CUSACK
PA

Three friends in their early-to-mid thirties. Cusack is well
dressed in fairly expensive outdoor-casual type clothes, Pa is
dilapidated, Barry is in between.

Setting

Outside Ennis, Co. Clare, Ireland. An almost abandoned building,
one main room, with a toilet, off, to the back. A dartboard on the
wall. Tape on the floor to mark the oche. There are several slabs
of lager and cider somewhere nearby and off, and a pile of about
two or three black refuse bags visible in the space. It doesn't even
have faded glamour, but there's something of a hermitage or
sanctuary about it.

Time

31st of May 2019 and, sometimes, seventeen years previously.

Notes

Some effort has been made to recreate an Ennis accent through spelling, etc. but it's not exhaustive, and rhythm is probably more important than specificity.

Lines given in square brackets indicate words not said, but meant by gesture.

's can mean an ellision of 'was' as well as 'is'.

'Ah', is a non-committed affirmative, a kind of 'Ya', without the Y.

'Sure' is usually the Irish discourse marker, with a very short stress.

Swearing is common but not stressed.

Finally, in the game on page 89–90, it probably won't be possible – either technically or in terms of stage time – to play exactly as written, so use the text there as a guide to how it should feel and what its outcomes should be.

This text went to press before the end of rehearsals and so may differ slightly from the play as performed.

ACT ONE

A dark and stormy night. Rattling branches, rain. Some white streetlight from outside barely lights the space.

CUSACK *enters, hurrying out of the weather. Can't believe no one's here. Sees* PA *passed out across the oche. Doesn't try to wake him. Looks further in to see if anyone is around, sees no one and so turns to leave.*

BARRY *enters from the bathroom, holding unlit candles, scaring the shit out of* CUSACK, *who in turn scares the shit out of* BARRY.

BARRY. Jesus Christ.

CUSACK. Who's there?

BARRY. Cusack? Is that you?

CUSACK. Sake, man, you scared the shit outta me.

What're you doing in the dark?

BARRY. Sure the lights [don't work].

You alright?

CUSACK. Oh I'm grand, ya, thanks Barry. I need to change my jocks like but I'm fine.

Is this everyone?

BARRY. Ya.

CUSACK. Just you?

BARRY. Well [and Pa].

CUSACK. Fuck sake, what happened?

BARRY. I dunno. He seemed grand when he came in. Bit wired.

You hardly have a light have you?

CUSACK. I hardly do. Is it drink just?

BARRY *rifles through* PA*'s pockets for a lighter. He finds one and starts placing candles around the place. The space grows more atmospheric. The dialogue continues throughout.*

BARRY. Dunno. He was delighted to see me, which was nice.

CUSACK. You shoulda known something was wrong so.

BARRY. Then he sat down. Next thing [he was like this].

CUSACK. At least he's here. Any word from the lads?

BARRY. No, I couldn't get signal.

CUSACK. Fucking Pointers, man. State a' the place.

BARRY. I thought I got through there from the sweet spot in the jacks but I haven't a clue could they hear me.

CUSACK. Show's your phone.

BARRY *shows his phone.*

Ya, surprised you don't need dial-up with that. Hang on.

CUSACK *takes out his (better) phone. Finds signal.*

Sake.

They're all in town. (*Shows* BARRY *the screen.*) Brodericks by the look of it. About… ten minutes ago.

BARRY. Pricks. They know what day it is.

CUSACK. Ya.

Sure…

BARRY. What?

CUSACK. We could head in there and meet'm.

BARRY. Ah we can't like.

CUSACK. Why not? Point of staying here when everyone's there.

BARRY. What if he wakes up?

CUSACK. He wakes up most days, I'm sure he'll cope.

Hmon – it in't his anniversary.

BARRY. Ah no. Leave it a while anyway.

CUSACK. Man, please…

BARRY. It's one evening. We can give him that.

CUSACK. One evening? I haven't been out since the birth.

BARRY. Anyway, they could be just having pints in town before they come out here.

CUSACK. D'you think?

BARRY. They said they'd come like. They know what day it is.

CUSACK. – .

They'd want to.

BARRY. D'you want a drink?

CUSACK. God ya. What do you have?

BARRY. Lots. Well, lots of cans.

CUSACK. I'll have a can so.

BARRY *gives him a beer. He opens it.*

To your holy soul and your swollen hole.

CUSACK *skulls the can.*

BARRY. You'll be fucked if you drink like that.

CUSACK. Promise? Gimme another one there. I've six months to make up for.

BARRY. No one made you stay at home.

CUSACK. No one made me? Aoife made me. D'you think if she's staying in I'm allowed out?

BARRY. You're out tonight.

CUSACK. Cos it's tonight. Game?

BARRY. Go on.

They start throwing darts, casually, though very well, without really keeping score.

She didn't want to come out with you?

CUSACK. Why would she?

BARRY. She knew him.

CUSACK *throws a dart a bit more emphatically.*

Same as all of us like.

She came with you before.

CUSACK. When?

BARRY. Last year?

CUSACK. No. She was five months pregnant last year.

BARRY. Year before then.

CUSACK. Sure someone had to watch the kid. We flipped for it
– she won a' course – then realised she hadn't expressed
enough milk to get through the evening.

Baby'd get some land if he latched, looked up and saw me.
(*Grabs his breast.*) Big and all as they are.

No Róisín either I see?

BARRY. Ya but Róisín never met him.

CUSACK. Ha? (*Tots it up in his head.*) Oh fuck ya.

It all blurs into one doesn't it? How long are ye now?

BARRY. Eleven years, give or take.

CUSACK. All just fucken blurs.

Suits you anyway.

BARRY. Are you messing?

CUSACK. No, seriously. What else would you be doing?

We're… seventeen. Fuck.

BARRY. Ya.

CUSACK. Believe that? Just over actually, off and on. Half our
lives. The kid not yet a year.

If we'd a' had our act together we coulda been finished
raising him by now. I'll be fifty before I sleep again.

BARRY. Is it bad?

CUSACK. He's a bollocks.

I'n waking up earlier too. Earlier than him even. Can't sleep expecting him to waken. I'd'be up I'd say half an hour before he stirs. He opens his eyes and I'n there standing over him.

BARRY. He loves that does he?

CUSACK. I know sure. Madness. One creak a' the crib and I'm like – (*Pulls a wide-awake face.*) It's gas.

Will ye have any?

BARRY. I dunno. We're young a while.

CUSACK. Not that young.

BARRY. I don't get on with most people I know. Not sure I should be adding to the problem.

CUSACK. Be grand. Telling you. Best thing about kids ya? Before I's always *thinking* about things. Worrying about work. Wondering should I upgrade the car or go to the gym more. If my arms were big enough or if we'd built the house the right way for the sun. And fighting with Aoife. You remember the way I was.

BARRY. Ya.

CUSACK. Well I tell you what. That stupid little prick of a kid means I haven't a fucken minute. He's always up in my face, crying or shitting or puking or laughing.

(*Smug.*) I haven't thought about *one* thing since he was born. Not one.

I'm busy, man. He needs me.

Ye should try.

BARRY. Ya.

Some stage, maybe. We're a bit busy like. Or she's busy. Work and stuff.

CUSACK. The new job?

BARRY. What?

CUSACK. Sorry. Like, Aoife told me. Ye must be delighted.

BARRY. Aoife told you? I only found out today. How did Aoife know?

CUSACK. Sure she knows everything. Róisín musta told her. They're always fucken texting.

If it wasn't for her I'd never get your news at all.

BARRY. Sake.

CUSACK. London though?

BARRY. Ya.

CUSACK. Class.

BARRY. Ya.

CUSACK. What?

BARRY. Ya, no, it's great. She's worked hard. There's exams there or something. She'll. Qualify. More, or. Whatever.

CUSACK. Don't blind me with the details anyway.

BARRY. Ya. Sure look.

CUSACK. You're going with her.

BARRY. What?

CUSACK. You're going with her I'm saying.

BARRY. Ya. Like. Obviously.

– .

What?

CUSACK. What did you do?

BARRY. What did I do? Why'd'you think I did something?

CUSACK. Man.

BARRY. Go on so; what did I do? You know more than me.

CUSACK. No, it's just. You can be a bit, fucken… moody.

BARRY. I'm moody?

CUSACK. You can be.

BARRY. And you're what the fucken Buddha?

CUSACK. No just built like him. What happened? Did you say something.

BARRY. No.

CUSACK. What?

BARRY. No, just.

Ah we'd a row driving over. I's late out of work. Last flight couldn't take off cos [the wind]

Then she was all excited. I still had the day on me, and she was like.

Maybe I didn't say anything straight away, or. You can't have a proper conversation in a car; she was driving, watching the road. Maybe she thought I wasn't saying anything cos… I dunno.

It's big news. She got annoyed. It's just weird timing. Good news on Liam's anniversary.

She dropped me off. I said I'll see her later.

CUSACK. You have to go with her.

BARRY. I am going with her.

CUSACK. Well. Fucken. Cheers.

BARRY. Ya.

CUSACK. It deserves a celebration.

CUSACK *skulls the end of his can and gets a fresh one each for him and* BARRY.

More than this.

BARRY. We're having dinner tomorrow. All the parents. Then leaving Sunday.

CUSACK. Jesus, two days?

BARRY. Ya she starts on Monday. She's the flat sorted and everything. She musta known for a while she was going to get it. Although she didn't say anything.

CUSACK. Maybe she didn't want to get your hopes up.

BARRY (*his hopes are not up*). Ya.

CUSACK. What are you going to do?

BARRY. Dunno. Haven't thought about it really.

They have airports don't they? I'll find something.

CUSACK. She didn't mind you doing this tonight?

BARRY. I was always doing this tonight. Why would she mind?

CUSACK. Dunno. Lots to do.

BARRY. Tonight's tonight like.

Are they still in town?

CUSACK *checks his phone.*

CUSACK. I think so.

BARRY. Pricks.

Seventeen years.

CUSACK. Ya.

BARRY. As long dead now as he was alive.

CUSACK. Shit; ya.

BARRY. – .

It'll be grand. She'll understand.

A flash of lightning maybe. Wind then silence. Then, groaning.

PA. Ohhhhh.

CUSACK. The fuck was that?

PA. Oh Jesus.

BARRY. Pa?

PA. Oh God. Cusack.

CUSACK. Fuck sake man.

PA. Cusack, is that you?

BARRY. Are you alright man?

PA. Oh no. Cusack. Oh no. I dreamt.

CUSACK. What is it man?

PA. I dreamt you weren't here. Fuck!

> BARRY *laughs*. PA *rises unsteadily*.

> I was lucky enough to sleep through you coming – I'd be never so blessed to pass out till you left.

CUSACK. I can go quick enough now.

BARRY. No. Come on.

> (*To* PA.) You alright?

PA. Kid.

> PA *is *fucked**. *He hugs* BARRY.

> I'n perfect. Here.

> PA *shapes to hug* CUSACK. CUSACK *is reticent, then relents*.

> PA *fakes out of the hug and catches* CUSACK *a nippy little pinch on the triceps*. CUSACK *jumps up to punch*, PA *stands in a defence pose*.

> What!?!

CUSACK. You prick.

> PA *relaxes out of the pose and puts a cigarette in his mouth. He's more composed than he was letting on*.

PA. How long's I asleep?

> *He's patting himself for his lighter. He doesn't have it.*

BARRY. Half an hour?

> BARRY *still has* PA*'s lighter. He lights his cigarette for him, then hands him back the lighter. There's a quizzical intimacy in this that can be played underneath the dialogue.*

PA. Fuck's everyone else?

CUSACK. We not enough for you?

PA. You're big Cusack, but you're not quite a crowd. Where are they?

BARRY. Brodericks, apparently.

CUSACK *starts browsing his phone.*

PA. Why?

BARRY. Think they might be having pre-pints before coming out here.

PA. Point a' that? There's about five slabs there. Tell'm to get their holes in gear.

CUSACK. They're not coming out.

BARRY. What?

CUSACK. Louise Duggan. Birthday drinks.

PA. Since when do we know Louise Duggan?

CUSACK. Since she married Aidan.

PA. Seriously? When?

CUSACK. Last year maybe? It's her thirtieth by the look of it.

PA. Show's.

Fuck sake.

Do you know her?

BARRY. Ya. She works with Róisín.

PA. Oh Róisín, ya, right.

Are they drinking champagne?

CUSACK. That's prosecco you gowl. As if they'd do champagne in Brodericks.

(*To* BARRY, *with a touch of the sommelier about him.*) It's not bad though.

PA. Fuck sake, fucken birthday drinks.

CUSACK. Just cos you weren't invited.

PA. Oh sure I'll weep into my pillow. They know what tonight is.

BARRY. Ya.

PA. Here.

Offers a toast.

To Liam.

BARRY. Liam.

PA. May everyone else get badly fucked.

They drink the toast.

CUSACK. And to Barry.

PA. Why to Barry?

CUSACK. Tell him.

BARRY. Róisín got a job.

PA. I thought she had a job.

BARRY. A job in London.

PA. Ah, shit one.

CUSACK. He's going with her.

PA. Point stands.

Sure grand. Ya. I'll drink to anything.

They toast and drink. PA *goes to the bags and takes out some drugs.*

Lads?

BARRY. No thanks Pa, not for the moment.

PA. Whatever. Sweetheart?

CUSACK. Man. I've a kid.

PA. You worried it'll come through in your milk?

Grand. Suit yourself.

PA *snorts.*

CUSACK (*about the black bags*). Is that all drugs?

PA. Yes, Cusack, that is the quantity of drugs I take on a Friday night. I go to the drug shop and ask for three bags of drugs please. Then I take them, and then I'm able for talking to you.

Snorts the other side.

It's my stuff.

CUSACK. What stuff?

PA. My stuff. Stuff I own. My things.

BARRY. Did something happen with Séamie?

CUSACK. Séamie?

BARRY. McCarthy. Landlord.

PA. Gowl. Got home from a house party about ten this morning, all that shit was outside. So I'm guessing he kicked me out.

I mean I hope he kicked me out. If he didn't he'll be fierce confused's to why I slashed his tyres.

CUSACK. What happened?

PA. Could be any number of things. I don't keep a diary.

BARRY. Where'll you go?

PA. When?

BARRY. Like. Where'll you stay? Going forward.

PA. Haha, what?

BARRY. Or. Tonight anyway.

PA. We're here tonight.

CUSACK. Not all night.

PA. Near enough. Five nice slabs to get through.

CUSACK. We're heading into town once we've done the thing.

PA. It's not just the thing. (*To* BARRY.) Aren't you coming walking?

BARRY. I've to meet Róisín. We've loads to do tomorrow before the flight Sunday.

PA. You said you'd come walking.

CUSACK. Walking where?

PA. You said.

BARRY. I only found out about London today.

PA. Fuck London you said *last year* you wanted to come next time. You said it last week.

CUSACK. Where are ye going walking?

PA *sulks*.

BARRY. I said to Pa I'd walk the road with him.

CUSACK. What road?

BARRY. The *road*…

CUSACK. Are you serious?

That's a motorway. You can't just walk on it. There are signs you spastics.

PA. It's grand. By time we're going. By time I'n going.

BARRY. What if I came back out after?

CUSACK. Ye'll be killed.

PA. Nah, it's always quiet at that stage.

CUSACK. How do you know?

PA. I can see into the future. (*Like he's having visions.*) Barry talks like a Tan, you're a fat lurk and there's no traffic on the bypass at four in the fucken morning.

CUSACK. Prick.

PA. I've done it before, obviously; it's tradition.

CUSACK. Fitting fucken tradition. Toner was an idiot to go walking the road that night and you're worse for repeating it. At least when he did it the road was closed and he was just a kid. You're thirty-odd and that's the M-18.

PA. It's grand. It's always grand. You'd know that if you weren't always leaving early.

BARRY. I can come back out once I've talked to Róisín.

PA. Forget it. I don't need you.

BARRY. She'll probably want an early night anyway.

PA. Ya she probly will. Who's she out with?

BARRY. Not sure.

CUSACK. Do you want a game Pa?

PA. You're grand. She at the 'birthday drinks'?

BARRY. Am. I'm not sure actually.

PA (*to* CUSACK). Show's your phone there.

CUSACK. Get your own.

PA. Shame she couldn't come out.

BARRY. It won't be a problem – honestly – I can / come back.

CUSACK (*urgent*). So what's the story with that airport job now man d'you've to hand in your notice like or what, must be weird?

BARRY. Am, ya, no, like I do, but. I've holiday built up and.

(*To* PA.) I could put in a word for you if you want.

PA. You're grand.

BARRY. It's handy work. You spend a lot of time outside.

PA. I spend time outside now; don't need work for that.

CUSACK. Plus he'd need a fixed address, hahaha.

PA. I could put down your mother's hole but no one'd believe I owned a place that big.

(*To* BARRY.) When are you off?

BARRY. Sunday.

PA. So today was your last day?

BARRY. No.

Shit; ya.

(*To* CUSACK.) I'd booked tomorrow off anyway cos of tonight.

I – ha. If I'd known today was my last day.

CUSACK. What?

BARRY. No.

> Just.

> It was a nice evening before the rain came. Orange and.
> The view from the runway there is class, all clear and low.

> I dunno. I'd a' paid more attention if I knew I wouldn't see it again.

PA. Girls Liam shifted.

BARRY. Aisling Moroney.

CUSACK. Marita Conroy.

PA. Laura McCauley.

BARRY. Olwyn Pearson.

PA. Oh ya!

CUSACK. Eimear Quinn.

PA. Abiola Okunrobu.

BARRY. Aoife Ryan.

PA. Haha.

CUSACK. Fuck sake.

BARRY. He did.

CUSACK. She's Aoife Cusack now.

PA. Time…

CUSACK. Am. Am.

PA. Time.

CUSACK. Sake.

> CUSACK *skulls a can as a forfeit.*

BARRY. Olwyn Pearson. Isn't she a model now?

PA. TV presenter.

CUSACK. Just TG4.

BARRY. Did he really?

PA. So he told me.

CUSACK. But you never actually saw him with her?

PA. No.

I actually saw him with Aoife though, if that helps.

BARRY *laughs*.

CUSACK. Fuck off the two of ye.

BARRY. When did they break up anyway?

CUSACK. Before the Leaving.

PA. Was it?

CUSACK. Ya.

PA. I don't think so. I think they were still together when he died.

BARRY (*sceptical of 'died'*). Ya.

PA. What?

CUSACK. She was with me. Before the Leaving even. Why d'you think I fucked it up so bad? Too much riding, not enough revising.

PA. How many points d'you need to be a builder?

CUSACK. I'm an electrician and more'n you'd think. How many did you need?

BARRY. Four-fifty.

CUSACK. How many d'you get?

BARRY. Three hundred.

CUSACK *raises his can to this achievement*.

I got it in the mocks. Just bad timing. First exam, World Cup on telly and your best friend in a coffin.

PA. Your 'best friend' was he?

BARRY. Whatever. They shouldn'ta had the funeral on the Wednesday.

CUSACK. Or the World Cup in the morning.

BARRY. They shoulda waited till the weekend. We coulda gone then.

PA. I went.

BARRY. I know you did.

PA. And I turned out okay.

CUSACK. Not like you'd a' done better if you'd sat the exams.

PA. Same difference wasn't it? Look at us now. Rising tide.

CUSACK. Speak for yourself.

BARRY. We all coulda gone is all I'm saying.

PA. Whatever. I went.

Beat.

CUSACK. Oh d'you see this? Top comment on the highlights. Last-minute goal against Germany, what's it say?

Read it.

BARRY. 'Bail that out u fuckers.'

CUSACK. Gas in't it? Bail that out. Cos of the bail-out? The recession like.

BARRY. I get it.

CUSACK. Savage.

Funny like.

Beat.

BARRY. Countries Liam'd been to.

CUSACK. Germany.

BARRY. Switzerland.

PA *doesn't compete, just skulls his can in forfeit.*

Don't think there was much more anyway.

Dropped out before the Rome trip, right?

CUSACK. School tours man. Class. D'you come to Rome with us?

PA. My hole. I hated school in Ennis, never mind going abroad.

BARRY. I couldn't believe he'd quit.

CUSACK. He was seventeen. He was allowed.

BARRY. Ya, but like. Why?

CUSACK. It was a hard year man. No shame being too weak to handle it.

PA. He wan't weak. He was never weak.

BARRY. What was it so?

PA. Fuck should I know?

He was just sick of it. Sick a' hanging out with ye pricks.

CUSACK. Musta been sick a' you an' all cos he din't take you with him.

BARRY. That year was shit in fairness.

CUSACK. Nah I loved it.

Loved the challenge.

PA. Cos you are challenged.

BARRY. What was it? Twelve-hour days.

PA. How was it?

BARRY. Half-eight at the gate; school till four then evening study. Home by nine for food and sleep. See the girls for twenty minutes at lunch if you were lucky.

And in between?

Fifteen-hundred lads.

Fucken smell a' mickey off the place.

Maybe he was right. Working. In the world. He got to spend more time with – girls like.

CUSACK *drinks*.

D'you think if it was a mixed school he might not a' left?

CUSACK. What's that got to do with it?

BARRY. Maybe if it wasn't all boys it all woulda been less hard.

CUSACK. Maybe you woulda been less hard.

PA *laughs*.

BARRY. You know what I mean. Maybe it wouldn'ta felt like such a fight every day.

CUSACK. I dunno. Stories Aoife tells it wasn't easy in the girls' school either.

BARRY. But if we were all together. Like primary school, girls and boys, if we coulda all just been friends, instead of caging us off like they were scared of us.

We were kids like. They were acting like we needed to be kept in quarantine.

If it was all a bit more normal maybe he'd a' never quit.

PA. It was just shit. It was designed to be shit. I'd say it was shit over in the girls' school too.

If we'd a' had the girls, you'd a' still been fucking pricks, just pricks that smelled a' Lynx.

I wouldn't go back if you paid me.

Course he fucken left.

BARRY. It's mad he was allowed just.

Like I couldn't wait to be finished but I'd a' never a' quit. I wanted to get *out*.

Last few months were electric, remember? Going around class saying what'd we'd applied for. These *careers*, supposedly. Like we'd apply, get in, and just *be* these new things, no hassle.

Professions like.

I started to think of everyone in terms of the courses they'd put down. Class full of architects, doctors, engineers.

CUSACK. What did you apply for?

BARRY. Art college. Graphic design. Make a fortune out of tech, obviously.

CUSACK. You?

PA. Fuck knows.

BARRY. You were science, all the way. Theoretical Physics.

PA. If I got the grant.

BARRY. Why wouldn't you have? We'd a' been in Dublin together. (*To* CUSACK.) You'd a' been dusted.

Woulda been cool.

CUSACK. Apply now sure. Must be hundreds of art colleges in London.

PA. There are art colleges in Limerick.

CUSACK. There's more in London. More of everything. You should.

BARRY. Sure I haven't drawn in years. It's all computers now.

Fuck sake I sound about a million years old.

CUSACK. Well. Whatever you want. London's massive, ye'll have a great time.

Will ye know anyone over?

BARRY. Am. [A] Few of the girls in Róisín's office transferred earlier in the year.

PA. No one you know, no?

BARRY. I think Barry Harrington's over. Him and Sonia Glynn.

CUSACK. Nah they moved back to Dublin. She's some architect now.

BARRY. Kevin O'Brien?

CUSACK. He's back too.

PA. Since when?

CUSACK. Christmas maybe? Robbed his housemates' rent, got the boat back overnight. Last thing I heard he was begging in Limerick.

PA. Fool.

CUSACK. Fucken sad like. Enny said he drove past him coming in from work.

PA. He didn't offer him a lift?

CUSACK. He's homeless. Where does he need a lift to?

BARRY. Well sure.

CUSACK. Ye'll be fine. Better off. Do yeur own thing. New start.

PA. And we could visit.

BARRY. You can if you want.

PA. Bring the lads. Enny, Aidan, Staples.

BARRY. Ah maybe not.

PA. Why not?

Do you not like them?

Does Róisín not like them?

BARRY. Nah, it's just it's just a one-bed. Be a bit small.

PA. The little one said.

BARRY. What?

PA. Roll over. Like. Three in the bed.

CUSACK *is very alert to* PA *now. Maybe he moves over and sits a bit too close to* PA.

Sharing with the lads.

BARRY. Ya like can you imagine?

PA. D'you know I can?

CUSACK *starts skulling his can, quick as he can.*

BARRY. But you'd always be welcome.

PA. Where would I sleep? In with you and her too?

CUSACK. Any more cans lads?

BARRY. There's loads. D'you want a beer?

CUSACK. Is there cider?

BARRY. In the back.

CUSACK. You ready for another one?

BARRY. Nearly; ya go on sure.

CUSACK. Sound. Get me one while you're at it.

Go on – I'm sitting.

BARRY. Sake.

Pa?

PA. You're very generous.

BARRY *goes to the back room.*

CUSACK. Fuck're you doing?

PA. Fuck am I doing?

CUSACK. He's going with her.

PA. Good luck to him.

CUSACK. So leave it.

PA. D'I say anything did I?

CUSACK. All that shit. Leave it now.

PA. Cusack, man, you'd want to relax. Blood pressure.

BARRY *comes back in, cans for the three of them; his own nearly finished one still on the go.*

BARRY. I thought of a good one there. Times Liam puked.

CUSACK. Easy. Pukahontas.

Slane.

BARRY. All Ireland Final.

Beat as we wait for PA.

CUSACK. C'mon man.

PA. – First day of school.

CUSACK. First day of second year.

BARRY. First day every year.

PA. When he shifted Aisling Moroney.

BARRY. Poor Aisling.

CUSACK. County final.

BARRY. Bus to Slane.

PA. The Queens.

CUSACK. Gracey's.

BARRY. Brodericks.

PA. Here.

CUSACK. Here times a hundred. Brodericks times a million. Karen Slattery's dad's car.

BARRY. Was he anorexic?

PA. Bulimic.

CUSACK. It's your go, stop messing.

BARRY. Am…

Fuckit.

BARRY *skulls a can as forfeit.*

CUSACK. There was nothing in that.

BARRY. It's the end of the one that's open.

That's the rules.

CUSACK. Fuck sake.

PA. The letter of the law isn't the spirit.

BARRY. Well unless you want *me* puking too.

CUSACK. Pussy baiy, Jesus.

BARRY. Letter of the law.

PA. Can't be helped.

I'll catch you again though.

BARRY. He wasn't really bulimic was he?

CUSACK. He was just a dirty bastard. I remember smoking with him at his house, out the side of the garage.

BARRY. The fucken garage!

CUSACK. And he took a big toke in his hand that way ya? Kept talking, but mid-sentence just turned his head and – blap – gakked into the flowerbed.

PA. You have that effect.

CUSACK. Piss off.

BARRY. Totally forgot about the garage. Man I loved that place.

CUSACK. Didn't we all. Shame we got thrown out though, ha?

PA. Fuck off.

BARRY. Why?

PA. He knows everything.

CUSACK. Tell him.

PA. We all smoked joints, Cusack.

CUSACK. We did. Not all of us were thick enough to flick our fucken roaches out the window.

PA. Whatever.

BARRY. Did his parents catch you?

CUSACK. Oh sure. His mam lost her shit. Wasn't even his stuff. Howard Marks here /

PA. HA!

CUSACK. flicking roaches out the back window. Dirty bastard skinning up seeds. One took root in the garden.

PA. Howard Marks. Where did you pull that from?

CUSACK. No one noticed till Liam and his father were clearing the lawn. In amongst the docks and nettles. Two-and-a-half feet of bould marijuana, hidden in plain sight.

BARRY. I did not know that.

CUSACK. Now.

PA. No one even got to smoke it. Gowls chopped it up for compost. Liam's mother wore a mask.

BARRY *laughs*.

CUSACK. What were they supposed to do? Dry it out and pack it for you.

PA. Woulda been nice. I never grew anything before.

CUSACK *laughs*.

BARRY. That's gas. I never knew why we stopped going to Toner's. I thought it was just cos this was better.

CUSACK. You think this is better?

BARRY. It used to be. Do you remember? Better [dart]board; we could smoke here. Drink. The girls used to come too. Not like being over at Liam's just stuck there with the lads.

PA. Ye should thank me so.

BARRY. Mad.

    – .

    Sure.

    – .

CUSACK. What?

BARRY. No.

    Just.

    We'd a' never come here. Would we? We'd a' never been out here but for that one small thing.

    He'd a' never a' come.

The accusation, soft as it is, floats in the air. BARRY is sorry to have taken this to PA, but it is what it is.

Beat.

PA. You know Róisín's riding Staples?

BARRY. – .

    What?

PA. You know your girlfriend there, Róisín? The one you're going to London with, ya?

CUSACK. Shut up Pa.

PA. She's riding Staples.

BARRY. Piss off.

PA. I mean – generally. Not like right now. Although [maybe right now].

BARRY. Are you taking the piss?

Is he?

PA. Why are you asking him? He told me not to tell you.

CUSACK. Shut up you prick, it's none of your business.

BARRY. Is he for real?

PA. It's a lot to process. Do you want some drugs?

BARRY. I don't want drugs for fuck sake; what the fuck are you talking about?

PA. Staples is riding / Róisín.

CUSACK. Shut up Pa. You don't know the whole story.

PA. I know the key points.

BARRY. Is he serious?

CUSACK *doesn't want to pull the trigger, but yes.*

BARRY *takes out his phone. Tries to ring Róisín, but can't get reception.*

Fucken thing.

Gimme your phone.

CUSACK. Don't man.

BARRY. Gimme your fucken phone.

CUSACK. I'n not giving you my phone. Relax a minute.

BARRY. I'n going to call her. If I've to walk into town to get reception, I'n going to fucken call her.

PA (*to* CUSACK). You wanted to go into town, didn't you? Watch the road though, won't ye?

CUSACK. No, come on. We're supposed to be doing this for Liam, aren't we?

(*Checking his watch.*) What time is it?

Come on. We're nearly there. Barry.

BARRY. – .

(*To* PA.) Give me drugs.

PA. Yes!

That is fine. Hmon.

PA *jumps into action and organises drugs, untwisting individual wraps. He doles to* BARRY *before taking a fresh one to* CUSACK.

No charge. No hard feelings.

BARRY *takes the drugs but the nauseous, restless need to respond to the news won't retreat.*

PA *offers the second wrap to* CUSACK.

CUSACK. No.

PA. Why not?

CUSACK. I told you. I've a kid.

PA. I'n not offering it to the kid.

BARRY. I'll be back in a second.

BARRY *goes to the toilet.*

PA. Loosen you up alright. (*Still offering to* CUSACK.) Be grand. Only a small one.

Hmon…

CUSACK. – .

Go on.

PA. Yes! Old times kid! Yes!!

CUSACK. Why do I do the worst things when I'm with you?

PA. Cos I'm the only one who'd forgive you.

CUSACK *snorts.*

Baiy the kid.

CUSACK. Jesus.

That's a bit [rough].

PA. In't it?

Killer?

CUSACK. Ya.

PA. Take a few warm-ups there. I'm just getting settled.

CUSACK. – .

You shouldn't have said anything.

PA. Ah. But I was always going to.

CUSACK goes to the dartboard and warms up his throw, while PA does exaggerated back stretches, etc. to let the drugs course through his system.

D'y'know, I was thinking I could start up like a yoga thing for speedheads. Instead of bells we'd have Enny on drums; instead a' tea there'd be little cups of Bucky. We wouldn't even need a Buddha, we could just get you to sit up front.

CUSACK. How much would you pay me?

PA. Not by the pound anyway.

You ready?

BARRY comes out of the toilet looking drugged up but baleful.

CUSACK. You alright? We're playing.

What?

BARRY. Sweet spot there for the signal, the jacks.

CUSACK. You phoned her?

Man. [You shouldn't have done that.]

PA (*taking one more little bump*). Yaow! That's the stuff.

Hmon. We ready? Closest to the bull.

He throws.

*

Liam Part I – spoken by BARRY

I'm not scared of anything. No, I'm not. My first day working
wash-up a knife slips off the counter and I catch it as it falls and
one of the chefs goes *Fuck sake Liam, a falling knife has no
handle, kid* and I was like *Ya but din't I catch it?*

I'm not a kid. And I'm scared a' nothing.

But sometimes something sort of tightens. The days ahead like
all stack up and fucken rush like mad and I go like tight inside
like a fist a fucken, it all comes haring torward me so I just

Get out of the way.

I'm in Brodericks now with the lads from work. Branko's head
porter; Kiss works sink like me. It's my going-away, so they're
buying me pints and making plans for the nightclub. I'm
standing by the door, holding my phone to the sky, trying to get
reception.

Sun's out but it's dark inside. Starting early but where are the
boys? It's supposed to be my send-off like. Barry, Cusack, Pa.
Who else?

Barry texts back: him and Cusack on their way, walking soon.
Pa wants to stay in Pointers cos he looks about twelve and he's
too cheap for fake ID but he has to come, they better make him.

I cop onto myself. Can't be staring into space feeling fucken
sorry. I don't regret it. No, I don't. Pa, Cusack, Barry, they've
their own shit going on. They're starting the Leaving next week.
And I'm leaving for good. Not even the oldest but they're all
still like schoolkids and I'm basically a grown man working, so.

LIAM KID WHAT'LL YOU HAVE Branko shouts. *PINT
PLEASE BRANKO BAIY.*

I never really quit school, I just stop going, so there's no big
moment there. I'm walking in one morning and the sun is pale
and rising like, well like the fucken sun y'know the way it'd'be

looking, and I'm there down here on the path all wet thinking *we've got double maths then English then results then applications then mocks then Leaving Cert then college then what then jobs then what*, and all I feel is all that weight a' days just haring for me so I tear off the side and walk instead to Pointers where I can chill and smoke and wait.

I do that one day. Then I do it another. Then I do it every day.

It's grand-out till the Mid Term when the report card lands at home. I'm sickened too cos I'd normally intercept but I'm dying coming down after being out all night with Pa, shrooming like and talking everything man, out all night we were, pure class.

Time I'm home though the tea's made, the envelope's open and the mother's at the table, burning fags to the filter going *Your father's coming to sort this out, Liam. Once And For All* she goes and I'm still half tripping so I'm like *once and for all Mam d'y'know like that's deep.*

He comes in and says nothing and I know I know it's bad but I'm hanging for sleep so I give it all up. Can't deny it, attendance shows one hundred per cent absence. Fully not there. Not one class or test for months.

My father, man. Mam's giving out, but Dad? I can see the weight of work. Things left on his desk. His prick of a boss and the long commute, knowing he's to get back on the road like now or get up early to make up the time. I'm on a To-Do list for him. Always have been. But it's a bigger picture.

They tell me about opportunities. They tell me anything is possible for us. We're lucky. Celtic Tiger like it's all for us. Mam makes tea. Gives me paracetamol. Can do anything I set my mind to. If they'd a tenth of the chances I have.

Whatever I want? Skulling pints in Brodericks. Darts at Pointers. Stalling with the boys in school. Then college. More classrooms, exams and jobs. Whatever I want. The world is wide.

I mean – I don't know what I want, do I? I don't have a clue what I want but I have a good strong fucken feeling it in't five-ten years of study, shut up and get on. For what? For some job? Come on. So you can beg your boss for an afternoon off cos your son's been acting the maggot.

Whatever I want. I pull a smoke from Mam's pack and spark it. *For fuck's sake* I say. *Fuck that*. She slaps me and leaves the room. The metal of her rings draws blood from my cheek.

She leaves her fags. They're halfway between me and Dad. He looks at the fag burning down in my fingers. I don't dare take a pull. But I don't stub it out.

I ask him if he has to go back in. He tells me to shut up. Doesn't shout. Doesn't smile. Five minutes later the fag's quenched and I'm not mitching no more. I'm typing up a CV on the utility room PC. LIAM TONER, Times New Roman, fourteen-font to fill the page. One life, single-sided. Dad drives me into town, drops me at Frankie Ryan's and goes back to smooth it out with Mam.

And all because I saw the sun and one day walked towards it.

We finish up in Brodericks quickly, Kiss's picking something up in Gracey's, so I text the lads again to say *I'm on the move like fucken text me*. It's daylight still but I'm kinda pissed already, the way the sunshine sort of cramps your eyes and you're like seeing in four dimensions whatever, and you say hello to the blue sky like you've spotted an old friend somewhere unexpected.

Branko thinks Frankie should come and buy a round or two. Kiss is like no though; to Frankie, the kid's not leaving, he's transferring. I'm the kid but I'm not a fucken kid. *But what about* us? Branko barks, like he's trying to pick a fight. Subaru Imprezas growl. Farmers in their townie cars. *What* about *us?* Kiss says, turning into Gracey's, he goes: *Fuck us*.

As if Frank Ryan'd come out for some porter he wishes he never fucken met.

Frankie Ryan owns the town, or so I've heard, or mostly. Three pubs, four restaurants, and the nightclub by the river. He's got hotels up the country too. Can't spend a wage in this town without some of it going in Frankie's pocket; even the new road out of town's being built across his land. Dad says Frankie's on some newspaper list of rich people and I'm standing like a fool with a one-page CV asking if he's any jobs going.

He doesn't know who I am. I tell him who my father is. He has me now. He likes my father so he ignores my CV and gets the car keys.

I don't know cars. Kiss is stone-mad for them and tells me Frankie drives an E-Class. He asks me about the engine noise but all that I remember is Frankie's laughter thickening as he's telling me about his schooldays with Dad. Best friends once, only my dad's not a millionaire, doesn't own a hospitality empire and isn't the guy whose land has been rezoned for the new motorway making him so instantly rich that the night he signs the contract he sits in Navan's for ten solid hours buying pints for whoever comes in while he cries his eyes out without interruption. My dad's none of those things. But he's the old schoolmate of the fella who is. Frankie Ryan. The boss.

He starts me in the kitchen. He means the sinks. Kiss Mongan showing me the ropes, same fucken day, me skagging still off the mushrooms, little scab on my cheek and elbow deep in suds and soapy food.

A falling knife has no handle kid, but here I am I caught it.

Getting busy now in Gracey's. I'm six pints in I'd say and I've had a nice few tokes with Kiss. Starting to fucken feel it. Eight o'clock. First streaks of orange dying red now in the sky. I check my phone and see ten missed calls. Loads of texts. Little envelope blinks in the corner of the screen. *No space for new messages.* It'll all just be the boys. I don't want to lose old texts just to make room for new ones.

I want them here. Not just the boys, like, everyone. I'm pissing every ten minutes, and I'm feeling like I might send a text I shouldn't. Make a call I shouldn't. Call her up and talk to see if there's room to change our minds.

Branko sees me maudlin and he touches the side of his nose. *One minute loverboy* he goes and goes off roaring laughing.

We laugh a lot in the kitchen man. Except when we're fucken roaring. *Where's my plates? Where's my pan? You fucken cunt why's this griddle greasy?* Because we're men we laugh and roar.

Kitchen's all men, so. I start off expecting them to take the piss cos I'm young, and I'm a drop-out but that's not rare, so I'm not that young.

No one asks what my plans are or what I want to do with my life. Here I am. Man now. Man like them. We laugh at the boys that work the bar cos it's easy work, and they laugh at us for the exact same reason.

Table-waiting's girls. Part-time mostly, still in school. I know the ones around my age, but the one everyone looks at is Aoife Ryan. Aoife I know too, just about. You can't miss her. Jesus, of *course* I know her. What I don't know though till Kiss whispers is that she's Frankie's daughter; his only child.

Aoife for reasons that are a mystery in fairness has zero fucken interest in me. It's pretty annoying. I've gone out with most her friends and we all still get on grand so. I dunno. Now and again I spot her up town with some fool like Anthony Redmond who's in a U2 covers band, called The Pro Bonos cos his dad's a solicitor. Three months they're together and I think it's even him that ends it. I remember the day I see them holding hands up town – Tony who's never had a girl to save his life and here he is starting with her and I think: that's criminal. Almost puts me off.

But I like the way she works hard, does the shitty jobs when she could get away with palming'm off, and how she laughs and jokes with everyone in the kitchen, even Kiss and even Branko.

It's weird.

I know there should be a defining moment. Some second I can point at and say that's when it changed.

She hates me first cos she thinks she knows me.

Defensive when she asks for cutlery.

But there's a thousand ways to hand a girl a fork.

A million ways to point a knife.

And if you time it well, and angle it right...

Like, girls are hard, but people are easy.

We're on a late together, but it's dead. Raining hard, no one eating. I'm out for a crafty fag by the bins and she comes out. Has her own pack. Good. Bad form for part-timers to bum off the full-time heads. Smokes near me. She doesn't talk.

And then she does.

She asks me what I'm up to after. I'm meeting friends, playing darts. She asks me where. I tell her about Pointers. Beyond the Rocky. She wants to come.

The Rocky Road is where they're putting the bypass. For now still though it's just this limestone crag on the outskirts of town. We pay Branko a tenner on top to get us two naggins before his shift starts. *Bold boy loverboy* he says in his Bosnian accent.

The rain has stopped and the clouds all clear. It's almost dark beneath the streetlamps. We hop the stile and walk the Rocky – it's still bright here without the lights.

We watch the light fade off the stones, under the late sun out to the new road under the old stars. We don't make it to Pointers. We shift the face off each other and it feels like forever and like we're in love.

Branko taps his nose again and shows the bag of yolks he's scored and we're nearly skipping down to the nightclub but it's new bouncers on the doors and no one knows'm personally so we're necking pills man in the queue and it's gas. I forget to worry about my fake ID so they don't ask me. Me and the men waltz straight in and like I'm nearly coming up before I hit the cloakroom, but I keep it just about together till I hit the noise and darkness.

Purple and green, spotlights, dark walls. Sticky floor, shitty music. Girls all in the centre, already bouncing. Boys at the edges, watching, waiting till they're hammered or a fucken slow song starts. We all know each other. Why do we wait?

It's a funny thing. The first time you look into another person's eyes and look to *see* – not what they think about you or not an explanation for why you feel what you feel about them but when you look at them because you want to see what's there. That's love, sometimes.

And when you feel it first you think – this is amazing, and –
I better never forget it cos I might never get it again.

And then you take drugs and discover you can feel the same for
some fool you usually hate for a fiver a pill. The world's a
funny place. I'm dancing in the nightclub, past the cloakroom
and the bouncers, dancing to music I don't like with people
I don't love and it's amaazing. I don't know where I am. I wish
the boys were here.

ACT TWO

*Later. Candlelight still. A game continues, but they're further
down their drugs by now. CUSACK is looser, intent on the
game. PA's about the same as before. BARRY throws
vigorously – he's furious, shaking his head in a small circuit
between throws.*

CUSACK. I don't know. Like. How much does it matter to you?

BARRY. What!?

CUSACK. It's one of those things, isn't it? It only matters if
you decide it matters. It's not like she's pregnant or anything.

BARRY. Fuck off.

CUSACK. Or sure dumping you? Like, she still wants you to
go to London.

BARRY. Man.

CUSACK. Nothing's changed.

BARRY. Seriously [shut up].

CUSACK. It's just – facts. You can forget facts. Or sure fucken
forgive.

PA. In his hole.

CUSACK. People forgive people. That's. It happens all over.

BARRY. Would you forgive it?

    If Aoife went with Staples.

CUSACK. Well.

BARRY. Ya.

CUSACK. I mean I'd have to have a think about it.

BARRY. *Staples*.

CUSACK. Hm. Hmm.

BARRY. Like.

CUSACK. I know sure. I get freaked any time she mentions Tony Redmond.

What can you do? The past is the past. Concentrate on now.

PA. She's fucking him now.

CUSACK. But that's like – nostalgia. She probly doesn't mean it.

PA. What the fuck are you talking about?

CUSACK. I just mean – it's always weird with exes.

BARRY. What exes?

CUSACK. Róisín. Staples.

BARRY. What?

CUSACK. They used to go out.

BARRY. When?

CUSACK. Ages ago. Before you.

Didn't she dump him to go out with you?

BARRY. What?

PA. How do you not know that?

BARRY. She used to go out with Staples?

CUSACK. Ya. Years ago. Not long but. A month or two?

Why'd'you think he doesn't like you?

BARRY. I didn't know he didn't like me.

PA. Fucking your girlfriend would be a good first clue.

CUSACK. Stop that.

BARRY. They were together?

CUSACK. For a while. Until she met you.

BARRY. I'd no idea.

PA. 'Ll'you stop shaking your head?

BARRY. What?

PA. I'n trying to throw darts here.

BARRY. Sorry.

> BARRY *shakes his head less.*

> How did you find out?

CUSACK. Aoife told me.

BARRY. Aoife knew.

PA. Everyone knew in fairness.

CUSACK. Ah Patrick. (*Using the long form signals a more sensitive/maternal* CUSACK *rising up out of the drugs.*)

PA. 'Patrick'?

CUSACK. What?

> Whose go is it?

PA. Yours.

CUSACK. Right. Sorry boys.

> *Make no mistake, these guys are amazing at darts.*

PA. How can you throw shaking your head?

BARRY. Am I shaking my head?

> CUSACK *nods a lot.*

CUSACK. It's like that time you had the yips.

PA. I never had the yips. I had the shakes in '03 but that was just the drink.

CUSACK. I got the yips with the baby.

PA. How can you get the yips with a baby?

CUSACK. Holding him.

PA. The yips is about fucking up your throw. Are you throwing the baby?

CUSACK. No, but I get nervous. Overthink the grip. Like before he could do his neck and that.

PA. What d'you mean do his neck?

CUSACK. Before he could hold up his head.

Jesus. D'you know nothing? Babies' heads are too heavy. So before his neck got muscle or whatever, his head'd be all over the shop. If you don't catch him right, you could drop him.

PA. What d'you do?

CUSACK. What?

PA. How d'you catch him right?

CUSACK. Oh. Well, you'd have him up in your arm so like his bum's inside your elbow.

PA *approaches* BARRY *and acts this out on* CUSACK*'s instruction.*

PA. Ya?

CUSACK. And your other arm goes up the back of him to hold his neck.

PA *does this.*

Ya. And the fingers just cradle the head.

PA *cradles* BARRY. *It's tender.* BARRY *stops shaking his head. Looks straight at* PA.

BARRY. Eleven years.

PA. Ya.

BARRY. Fucken.

Okay things aren't. Things aren't always.

It's hard, whatever.

But this?

PA. Ya.

BARRY. How could she?

PA. She's a bitch.

CUSACK. Don't.

PA. What?

(*To* BARRY.) That's what you said. When you started going out with her.

BARRY. Eleven years ago.

PA. You said she was a bitch, and a headwrecker and you wanted nothing to do with her.

BARRY. I just meant I liked her.

PA. Ya but that's the same thing that's in her now.

CUSACK. He's right man.

BARRY. I didn't think that meant /

I can't stop picturing /

Fuck!

Doesn't matter now.

CUSACK. What did you say to her?

BARRY. I said I hoped she was having a good night.

I said she should say hello to Staples and that I wasn't coming to dinner tomorrow.

CUSACK. That all?

BARRY. I called her a cunt.

CUSACK. Ah.

PA. What did she say to that?

BARRY. Voicemail.

CUSACK. Probably still out at the party.

BARRY. Fuck am I going to do?

PA. Nothing. *She*'s leaving. *You*'ll be grand.

BARRY. What?

PA. Keep the head down it'll be over by the weekend.

CUSACK. Well.

BARRY. What?

CUSACK. It won't will it? There'll be a million conversations yet. Texts. Chats. Explaining to your parents. Seeing her parents in town.

They won't thank you, like. You'll be the reason they found out their daughter likes it up her.

BARRY. Oh Jesus.

CUSACK. Or.

BARRY. What?

CUSACK. You could forget about it.

PA. Are you for real?

CUSACK. Pa. In relationships. These things happen.

PA. Riding other people?

CUSACK. It happens.

PA. People like Staples.

CUSACK. To each their own.

PA. He called her a cunt.

CUSACK. Ya, you'll probably have to say sorry for that.

Although, I called Aoife a cunt the other day, no, yesterday?, and it was grand.

BARRY. Why?

CUSACK. I dunno. The kid was crying. I was tired. She was probably being a cunt.

Checks his phone as he talks, thinking of home.

Like Aoife once boxed Orla Fox for calling her rich, but she didn't even blink when I said that.

So she might get over it.

BARRY. Aoife's sound though.

CUSACK. Maybe Róisín's sound. Or sound enough. Give her a chance.

PA. That's bullshit.

CUSACK. You don't know man. Inside a relationship? Fuck knows how we hold together.

Few more days you'll be in London. Fresh start.

PA. He's not going to London now.

CUSACK. Why? Did she say you can't come?

PA. He barely wanted to go before – he can't go now.

CUSACK. You don't know I'm saying.

Fresh start. Telling you. I wish we'd managed it. Get away from everything.

BARRY. From what?

CUSACK. Everything. That happened. That people know about us.

It took us years to.

Get right. Over things.

BARRY. What things?

CUSACK. Cos. Being. Like, her dad and. How we started.

Like.

I just mean everyone has a past, everyone has things that happen, you just fucken get over them, you don't have to make them the centre of everything or the end of everything.

Easier do it if you get away.

BARRY. Why didn't you?

CUSACK. We nearly did actually. Australia. Coulda been class.

PA. When?

CUSACK. After the apprenticeship. I'd saved a bit.

BARRY. Australia?

CUSACK. Ya. Work lined up with my cousin. Visas, everything. But Aoife hadn't the money.

PA. Aoife Ryan didn't have money?

CUSACK. Frankie wouldn't give it to her. Said she could have it for a deposit. But he wouldn't waste it on travelling.

So we bought the house.

Ha. Keys in April. Moved-in May. Two months later, sure the banks [collapsed], and now we can never fucken sell it.

House-warming that summer was like a fucken wake.

BARRY. That's where we met.

CUSACK. At my house?

BARRY. That party. Chatting by the fridge. Shifting in the garden.

Moved into the flat what, three months later?

I'd been planning on going back to college. Teaching. But then.

Everyone was like 'don't give up a job'. Teachers emigrating, hiring freeze. And she was on good money. So we got the flat in town and I stayed on at the airport.

I saw so many people flying out. Mothers crying. Rucksacks. Felt like I was dodging bullets.

PA. Course you were. Fucken point a' leaving?

BARRY. To like, do better.

PA. Better what? Name anyone who left. Mark Ryan: got a job, got a girl, paying rent. Barry Harrington: got a job, got a girl, paying rent.

CUSACK. Sonia actually owns their house so.

PA. Spancil? Fair play, he's gay now, whatever, but he's still signing on over, gets less than I do here.

Point a' that? Where he knows no one and no one knows nothing about him.

CUSACK. Better'n being stuck here.

PA. Is it? Why are they all dying to come back so? Posting old pictures, playing remember-me-this. Fucken obsessed with shit that happened years ago.

BARRY. As if we're any different.

PA. We're still here! That shit's *ours*. That's us.

CUSACK. We shoulda left.

PA. You'd a' only come back.

CUSACK. No man. If she'd come too?

    But he paid her to stay. Said I could enjoy Australia on my
    own. Go to fucken Antarctica if I wanted. Told her he'd buy
    her the house outright.

    I wouldn't let her take the money.

PA. You took the deposit quick enough.

CUSACK. That's a loan. I'll pay that back.

PA. You will ya.

CUSACK. I fucken will.

    Prick is all he is.

    Stuffs away his phone.

PA. Your own fault baiys.

BARRY. How is it?

PA. Had to go moving in. Had to go getting houses.

BARRY. We live in a flat.

PA. Acting all domesticated. Garden centre. Mortgage,
    whatever. 'Magine falling for that.

BARRY. And what?

PA. What?

BARRY. What's your fucken secret so if you're such a genius?

PA. At least I avoided it man.

BARRY. Cos no one'd have you.

PA. Do my own thing. Want to stay in, I stay in. Want to go out,
    I go out.

BARRY. You do. You and your three soaking rubbish bags.
    Your drugs.

PA. Drugs you take.

BARRY. Your years signing-on, acting like you've cracked it. Like you got it right, and we're fucken eejits for trying to make a go of it.

PA. A go of what?

BARRY. Look at you now, getting it right. Nowhere to live and totally alone.

PA (*angry*). Two of us in it kid.

Beat.

CUSACK (*softly*). What happened with the gaff you were renting from Séamie.

PA. Fuck Séamie. Gowl.

CUSACK. How long were you there?

PA. Year. Two maybe.

CUSACK. So ye musta useda get on. Maybe if you apologised.

PA. For what?

CUSACK. For whatever you did.

PA. I did nothing. He can apologise to me, my fucken things all soaked. I only went to his house for a reference.

BARRY. For what?

PA. For nothing.

For a job.

Fucken, Tesco thing.

BARRY. Ya?

CUSACK. What happened so?

PA. Ask him. I was whatever, polite, everything. Cycled out with two naggins in case his girlfriend was home.

BARRY. They're married.

PA. Whatever the fuck she can still fucken drink can't she?

CUSACK. Go on.

PA. Nothing, fucken, just we're just sitting there, me and Séamie, watching telly. Me on the two-seat, him on the recliner. What was it, fucken *Bondi Rescue* or something. *Animal Planet*. I dunno.

Drinking handy cos I've to ask a favour. But he won't touch a drop. Says he's grand. Shows me this fucken smoothie he's gulping. Litre of it on the floor next to him. Colour of gawk or burger sauce. For his nuts, he goes.

BARRY. What?

PA. Serious. Like something he'd drunk yesterday and wanted to taste a second time.

CUSACK. I had that. Banana, walnut, goji. Ups your count supposedly.

BARRY. Ya?

CUSACK. Looks like puke but it only tastes like shit so [it's not too bad].

PA. He's slurping like a calf, telling me science about his balls. Shows me a calendar. Ovulation schedule. Fuck sake. But I had to listen didn't I? If I wanted him to sign the thing.

Next thing herself comes in. Steaming, chewing on a penis-straw. Hen party. Flaming. But delighted to see me.

Maeve Russell. McCarthy now. I forgot I fucken knew her; same estate where Mam's house was. We went to the same primary like. She was sound, for a seven-year-old. Good at Maths. Nicer'n me. Moved out before we started secondary. Her parents bought a proper house or. All-girls school out the country.

She drops beside me on the couch. Starts on the other naggin. Telling us about the party. Good craic like. Remembering me some shit about communion or, I dunno. Funny shit.

Next thing, Séamie ups and fucks off. I thought just the jacks, but nah. Ten minutes, twenty, no sign. Maeve has me skinning up, doing her old townie accent, but it was nice too; she's sound like, and she *was* from there, so she *is* from there. I din't mind really except it was like two in the morning, if Séamie dun't come back I'n going to have to camp out there all night.

'Bout three he comes in. Baggy pyjamas, thick head. I was stocious. He's there t'me like 'what am I still doing?' I say about the signature. So he signs it. 'Now, fuck off.' Fair enough. I try and stand, but fall back onto Maeve. She's pissing herself laughing, starts tickling me.

I don't think I'll be able to cycle. I ask Séamie for a lift. He doesn't seem keen. Maeve says I can sleep on the couch. That sorts it. He gets his keys.

We go out, cold enough now, throw the bike in the back of the van. Freezing like. Pyjamas pure draughty. He goes back in for a coat.

I's out there ten minutes I'd say. Getting cold. Getting sober. Back door closed. I go around to the bedroom. He's there, raging at her. Holding up his calendar. And she's laughing. Just laughing, chewing her straw. 'You're ovulating' he says. 'Look! Look!' Pointing at the calendar.

So she just starts, like, going at him, y'know. In under the pee-jays. Still laughing. Soft hands though, so it's working. And even though she's laughing, she's like 'Come on so, Daddy.'

BARRY. Are you serious?

PA. I could hardly believe it. My fucken lift.

CUSACK. Ah, it's a balls trying to manage those schedules. You've only a very short window. They've been trying for ages.

PA. I wasn't going waiting for ages. I had to get my bike.

I looked to see if there was a spare key. There wasn't, but at least I looked, ya?

I smashed the back windscreen, got the bike and cycled home. Took me twice as long as usual. I's probly riding on the zigzag.

BARRY. Did you really smash his windscreen?

PA. Don't be looking at me like that; fair's fair, he said he'd drive me. Was I meant to walk?

BARRY. You're walking tonight.

PA. I am, but it's not as far. You're free to come now too.

CUSACK. Can I come? I'd like to come. I feel like it now like.

BARRY. Why'n't you knock on their bedroom window?

PA. I didn't want to – like – bother'm. In their... (*Does he sentimentalise the love he saw?*)

CUSACK. You fucken romantic.

BARRY. Have you been talking to him since?

PA. Séamie? I'll *be* talking to him. Musta left them [bags] out all night. Clothes, books. Soaked.

CUSACK. You should hang up the clothes. Spread out the books to dry'm.

PA. Fuck it.

CUSACK. It'll make all the difference. (*Gets up to do the laundry.*) Will you get your deposit back?

PA. As if I paid a deposit.

CUSACK. That's handy.

BARRY. How much was the rent?

PA. Two hundred. When I paid it.

BARRY. It was. A week?

PA. A month.

CUSACK. What?

PA. I think.

CUSACK. Two hundred a month?

PA. Ya. It was a shithole like. Wan't worth much more.

CUSACK. Jesus.

Our mortgage is eight hundred apiece.

PA. Ha!

CUSACK. Bills another hundred. Baby 'bout four for food and nappies.

Our food, the two cars, college loans, and the holiday there the other year. 'Nother three a piece.

What's that? Two and a half, three grand? Before we even think of saving or buying a drink. Working three weeks in the month just to cover costs.

And that's if she goes back to work. Man.

PA. Ha.

CUSACK. What ha?

PA. Just like.

I'm probably worth more than you.

BARRY *laughs*.

Clear ten grand signing on.

Per annum, d'y'know?

CUSACK. Fucken hell.

She doesn't need to live like this. Watching the month. Frankie'd have bought the house for her. Still would, if she asked him.

She doesn't need me. What I earn? She doesn't. Minute she changes her mind.

BARRY. Why would she?

CUSACK. Why wouldn't she? Nothing keeping her. She can afford to leave me.

BARRY. She's not with you for the money man.

PA. Not the looks either.

CUSACK. Then what?

What am I doing? So much work to work out even. What're we doing?

PA. Maybe you *shoulda* left so.

BARRY (*to* PA). What'll you do?

PA. I dunno. You'll need a room-mate won't you?

BARRY. Ha.

Oh – (*Realising.*)

CUSACK. What?

BARRY. – . She earns more'n me. Pays more than half the rent.

Pained beat.

I can't afford the flat on my own.

CUSACK. Oh.

BARRY. I'll have to move back to Mam and Dad's. I'll have to go back to the airport.

PA. Sure you never left.

BARRY. I'm so fucked.

PA. You haven't even given notice.

BARRY. I was finished though. In my head? I was gone.

Like I wasn't sure if I wanted to go but I knew I was fucken going.

It's like those ghost stories or science fiction whatever. Where the fella goes away for forty–fifty years and comes back and feels older. But no time's passed where he left.

PA. That's not science fiction.

BARRY. Whatever.

PA. That actually happens.

BARRY. What?

PA. Speed of light shit.

CUSACK. He's right.

PA. Twins. Einstein. Look it up.

BARRY. All those years we've been together. How far did I get? Nowhere. Back to where I started.

How can I start again?

PA. What time have we?

CUSACK (*checks time on phone*). Shit. Two minutes.

PA. Right.

PA *rushes to get the cans.*

CUSACK. C'mon.

BARRY. This is bullshit man. This is all.

We're remembering a kid. Who did nothing. Didn't finish school, didn't finish anything. Lies down one day and fucken kills himself.

CUSACK. Ssh.

BARRY. Fucken got away with it.

CUSACK. Stop man. Just.

PA *re-enters with cans. Probably heard what* BARRY *said but doesn't engage.*

BARRY (*to* CUSACK). How long have you known?

CUSACK. A while.

BARRY. Why didn't you tell me?

CUSACK. I thought Pa would.

BARRY (*to* PA). Why didn't you tell me?

PA. I did tell you.

BARRY. Why not sooner?

PA. I thought you knew.

BARRY. What?

PA. She was always a prick to you man. And you took it.

You put up with everything else. I figured you were putting up with this too.

I din't want you to have to admit it.

This is plausible.

BARRY. I'm tired.

Have you more?

BARRY *gets more drugs off* PA. CUSACK *gets more too.*

Are we playing?

PA. Right. Yes. We are gathered here today.

BARRY. Come on man.

CUSACK. Let him.

PA. We are gathered here today to honour the memory of Liam Toner. Who died on this night.

BARRY. Or thereabouts.

PA. Seventeen years ago. We honour him in the traditional fashion, with a solemn game of Pointypukes.

BARRY. Was that really the name?

CUSACK. Ssh!

PA. Hit a twenty, drink to twenty, nineteen – nineteen [etc]. Hit a double, half the time; treble, last man drinks. Bull, we drink for fifty; outer, you for twenty-five. Miss the board, that's a minute. Ya?

CUSACK (*checking his phone*). Cans to see who goes first?

BARRY. There's no advantage going first.

PA. But there's every advantage in a can.

To Liam.

The three skull cans. BARRY *gives up first. Then* CUSACK. *This is second nature to* PA.

CUSACK. Brgh. Pa's first.

They begin to play the game, but after the first round or so, CUSACK*'s phone rings.*

PA. Leave it.

He answers, the game is interrupted.

CUSACK (*to phone*). That is so weird! I just took out my phone to see if you'd texted. Ya. Just now.

PA. Sake.

CUSACK. Is everything alright?

Really?!

He crawled?!

Oh my God!

No, I'm grand. Hang on a second.

He's crying.

I'll be home. I want to see him.

No. I swear.

Send me a video, will you?

He is really crying.

I'll talk to you later. I'll see you soon. I'll text you from the taxi.

He hangs up.

What is wrong with me? He's crawling. Why am I crying?

PA. Your hormones?

CUSACK. This speed is weird.

PA. MDMA.

PA *throws a dart.*

CUSACK. What?

PA. You took MDMA. C'mon are we playing.

BARRY. No – really?

CUSACK. Why aren't ye crying so?

PA. We took speed. You took MDMA. Lads, the time?

CUSACK. What the fuck is MDMA?

PA. It's grand. It's nice. It's drugs.

BARRY. Fuck sake, man.

CUSACK. How long will it last?

PA. I dunno. It's basically Ecstasy.

CUSACK. I've never taken Ecstasy.

PA. How is that possible?

CUSACK. I hate dancing. Why'd'you give it to me?

PA. Jesus Cusack. You're aggravating at the best of times.
    You'd a' been a total dose with speed inside you.

CUSACK (*scared*). Patrick!

BARRY. You'll be okay man.

CUSACK. No. I want to go home.

PA. We're playing, c'mon.

CUSACK. He's crawling. He never crawled before. Why'm'I
    FUCKEN CRYING!

BARRY. Come on Cusack, calm down.

PA. Have a can.

BARRY. That'll be worse.

PA. Not really. They're different things.

CUSACK. Show me.

   CUSACK *drinks a can really quickly.*

PA. There. You're grand. It's your throw.

BARRY (*to* CUSACK). Are you alright?

CUSACK. I don't feel right.

BARRY. What are you doing?

CUSACK. I'm going to puke it up.

PA. You snorted it. You'd be better off sneezing.

CUSACK. Will that work?

PA. No.

CUSACK. This isn't right. I'm going to / [go vomit]

>CUSACK *runs outside.*

BARRY. Cusack!

>Fuck sake Pa.

>BARRY *rushes out after him.*

>PA *in the space alone. He throws a dart, drinks the time.*

>*The lights comes back on. Glaring flickering fluorescence. The spell is totally broken, disgusting* PA.

PA. Agh.

>BARRY *comes back in, wet from the rain.*

>Lights are working.

BARRY. I couldn't give a shit Pa. He's fucken gone.

PA. Sure off with him.

BARRY. Haring up the road.

PA. Soft piece a shit.

BARRY. He's freaking out.

PA. Sake! It was a tiny bump, the size of him.

BARRY. He hasn't been out in months. You coulda given'm a heart attack.

PA. Fat prick's got more chance of a heart attack from running than he has from me.

>BARRY *leans in towards the toilet, his phone to his ear.*

BARRY (*to phone*). Can you hear me?

PA. What're you doing?

BARRY. Ya, town please. Just off the motorway. Junction 11, first right heading south. How long'll you be?

>Sound. I'll meet you on the road.

PA. What're you at?

BARRY. Thanks. (*Hangs up.*) What am I at? I'm fucken going after him.

PA. Will you come back?

BARRY. I dunno.

PA. I need you / for

BARRY. I'll see, I said.

PA. Fuck sake! Fuck actual fuck sake! It's his anniversary! Am I the only one that gives a shit?

BARRY. No man. You're just the only one that gives a shit in this one particular way.

One night remembering someone who got himself killed years ago.

I'n gonna go make sure another one doesn't get himself killed tonight.

PA. My hole.

BARRY. If I'm not back later, I'll give you a shout over the weekend.

PA. Go if you're going you fucken pussy piece a' shit go fuck yourself.

BARRY. Grand, ya.

BARRY *nearly exits.*

PA. Can you leave me the keys?

BARRY *doesn't.*

BARRY *leaves.*

Sake!

PA *smashes the fluorescent bulb. Darkness.*

Interval.

Liam Part II – spoken by CUSACK

I think I might be out of my mind. A bit. But that's alright.

I'm on my own. The boys aren't here, pricks. The *lads* are though, the *lads* from *work*, Branko, Kiss, they came out, this is where I am now.

Fuck the boys for not coming. Liam Toner, party of one.

The dancefloor's chaos, that good chaos I love. Fellas jumping, knees locked, arms around like they've won a match; girls unsteady, legs wrecked from dancing every song. Everyone drinking to keep up with everyone else.

I'm on the ceiling and I'm glad it's there cos without it I'd be in the sky.

Down here at the dancefloor's edge, Branko's talking Kiss's ear off like they're picking who they're after. I can't hear what they're saying. Toss up whether they're looking for a fight or a shift. I don't know'm well enough to know which one they'd prefer.

Pa'd rather fight than shift, shy little fucker. Barry'd rather go home. Cusack'd take whichever like just take it as it comes.

I should float on over to them. Maybe. They might be up in Brodericks. They might be with a crowd.

I cross the dancefloor, just cross and walk, I'm going to go and see my friends, but I hear my name out loud.

Liam.

Liam Toner?

Who?

Who's that talking to me?

Maeve. Fucken Maeve Russell.

She comes right up to my ear and says it again; I nearly feel, sort of taste the tongue of its 'L', the beam of its 'ee', the nuzzle of its 'M'. *Liam* she goes, my name in her mouth.

I know Maeve since primary, but we're not close since. Try and kiss her when we're seven, lining up for First Confession. She isn't having it, runs away, rats me out. What about now? She likes me now, I'd say. Music thumps; she puts her arms around my neck and my guts jump. Right.

Her mouth's all warm. I remember her winning races on Sports Day. Boys and girls all in together. She's arms and elbows, red cheeks, ponytail flying left and right. Damie Rynne's steaming, loves being fastest, plus losing to a girl; him and his silver medal, raging. But he does lose. And she wins.

She wins and now it's years later and I haven't seen her since they split us up for secondary. Is she still the same? Walks right up and kisses me out of nowhere like it hasn't been an age.

Aoife's mouth is always cold, like chewing-gum, and ice from her fridge, little thermos bottle.

I kiss her like I'm thirsty, like everywhere's a desert.

I mean it man. No messing. We're seventeen and we have it.

And who cares about the stories? There's always stories.
A thousand warnings, a million reasons to avoid it. But I don't.

She comes haring towards me and I don't get out her way.

I mean I know, 'Don't be going with the boss's daughter.'
I know that. Everyone knows that, everyone says.

But I do, obviously. Not because she's the boss's daughter but because she's Aoife. Because she loves me and.

I clean up Pointers. Tell the boys to stay away. Buy a little lock so no one interrupts. Make the place look nice; curtain on the window, sweeping up the floor. Tape-player that runs on batteries. Cover the dartboard in like pictures of her and me together. Buy a *shitload* of candles and two spare lighters.

I do it all. And we go together, across the Rocky, we make it there and it feels like home.

No one interrupts. We even doze a bit afterwards; I keep waking up at every sound, but I nearly sleep a while as well. I've never known anything like it. We set an alarm, get up, get dressed. Aoife gives me a kiss.

I have to fix the place back afterwards or else the boys'd rip the piss, so I do and then we go to hers. She's ripping me too cos her house's empty all day – parent–teacher meeting, but she's smart so she's not worried. Still she likes the effort I make, the thought I put in to it, I can tell.

The lights are on when we arrive at hers. I'm nervous; her mother likes me cos mothers like me. I've never met her dad outside a' work. I've no idea what he knows. But he likes my father, so?

They're in the kitchen when we come in. Nice fucken house. They've been arguing though.

Frankie's red in the face. Not expecting me. The sudden silence, like my ears've fallen off. You can see him confused cos he knows me but he nearly can't place me away from the restaurant.

He has a report card in his fist. Shaking like a heart. And a look like he's just worked out what's what.

A million reasons. Not the boss's daughter. But sure what can you do about love?

Aoife's mother goes hello and in one breath says I must call again. I don't take off my jacket, just goodnight, some other time. I see through to the kitchen as the front door closes. Aoife dun't look up.

She wants to be a doctor. She's fucken smart enough. But in the last few months, her classwork, her homework. Me. The results are slipping, and she's lucky if she gets nursing.

All the things we learn and feel and do together count for nothing when they're deciding what she's worth.

She's not in work the next weekend. Or the weekend after. Someone says she's gone. Different school, down in Limerick. Grinds and extra classes.

I leave it a week, but. It's the usual thing. Isn't it? No credit, no calls; some credit, no answer. One day, a letter. She agrees with her parents. She wants to do well.

A new job comes up up the country. More money, accommodation. I'd be cooking. Do I want it? Or do I want to stay? I don't have to decide yet. Just apply for the job and see if I get it.

I get it.

Still kissing Maeve as the music slows down. I'm trying to keep my head here now now look that's Maeve but I'm floating away. It's not that I'm not into it but she's got me close so she can tell something's missing. She breaks away and I let her go but she takes my hand and leads me to the bathrooms so I go that way instead.

I lean against the stall, rattling the lock. Maeve stands in front of me, facing away. She reaches down, crooks her hand below her skirt. Beyond the door some girls are laughing, shouting at the mirrors. I can see the sky blue of Maeve's underwear as she lifts her leg to reach. I start fumbling at my zip I suppose, but she laughs when she sees what I'm at. *Hang on a sec* she goes and takes out a small bag of powders.

The Ketamine drops from my nose to my throat. I try and swallow between kisses. This is not my first confession. Maeve presses against me, her hand is soft inside my fly. Her skirt is velvet and the scrape makes my teeth drip. Can my hand bend round that way? Her underwear is softer, looser. I haven't a fucken clue what I'm doing, she feels like someone else. She takes my hand and holds it steady and moves herself around it. I remember the thing about sitting on your hand until it's numb. It's good to get away from yourself.

Oh. Here it comes. I love it when this happens.

I'm far away. I'm above the stalls. Above the lights, inside the cistern. My ears are porcelain. I can't even hear. Maeve clamps and breathes. That's Maeve. Where am I?

Right now I'm in the ladies' toilet in a nightclub with a girl.

But I'm also fifteen in the garage smoking, throwing darts with Pa.

And there I am too a month or so ago and back at work talking to Aoife for the last time.

I'm in all three at once. And three things happen together.

I'm in the kitchen covering someone else's shift. Aoife comes in and stops in her tracks. Her eyes dart to the roster. We've not been on together since that night, but it's not me who's picking my shifts.

And I'm there in the kitchen forever but I'm fifteen too in the garage tossing roaches, talking shit. Pa's nailing shots. Hits 140. My eyes are raw.

And I'm in the kitchen and I'm in the garage and in the toilet too with Maeve shifting my face off, off my face and everywhere. Is this what I want?

Aoife comes over for cutlery. I let her take it. I don't look at her. I don't know if she looks at me. I wonder if our eyes away we're both looking at the same thing, the same puddle of water on the same bit of floor.

She says congrats on the job. Says I'll make chef in no time. Looks annoyed. I ask if she's applied to college. She has. Where? Other side of the country from where I'm going. If she gets in. I tell her good luck. But it sounds like I mean goodbye. G'd'luck. G'luck.

She looks annoyed. I can't ask why. And when I tell my parents about the job, my mother cries and my father doesn't. But are we all thinking the same thing? Maybe I don't go? Maybe she doesn't get in?

I should have said all this. I should have said something more.

And in the garage years ago Pa's saying he read something. I laugh. He hits me for laughing. Says time is a dimension. Like height. And we're points on a line. Time doesn't move man. It just is.

I need to sit down. I toss my roach out the garage window. What, like everything *is*. Everything that ever happened, happens, will happen.

But I dunno. There's still before and. Before I don't go to school and after I start work. Before I text the boys and after I kiss someone else. Before I met her and after I leave forever. It all *is*, but some of it's finished and the rest is yet to come.

That's just a load a' words Pa goes, but I don't know what that means.

Aoife looks away, Pa laughs I don't know why, and Maeve's close and nearly there. She's making noise and finishing up and the girls outside are laughing. When she's done they all cheer and whistle. She fucks them out of it but they don't give a shit.

They tell Maeve to hurry on so they can fucken piss so she fixes herself and pushes me out. The girls at the mirror don't seem to see me. Maybe I'm not here. Maeve walks and I follow, skipping over the water pooling on the ground, like stones, sliding.

She gets to the bar and calls two tequilas. We slam them back and take the taste from our mouths. She kisses me again then one last time. I feel good don't I? I don't feel bad.

I nearly ask her for her number cos it's not like I've no manners, but she sees it coming and laughs. Says she has a boyfriend basically, she was only kissing me to prove a point. What point I go? And she says about me running away from her when she kisses me at First Confession. Me running away from her? That's not how I remember it. But she seems sure. She laughs and hugs me and gets swallowed by the crowd, ponytail bopping left and right. I feel an imprint of her hug on my chest but I'm floating somewhere else now too.

I get it. For a second I see it all like from a distance. I shouldn't let it end like this. I should tell her, Aoife. Tell her I get it. She wants things to be right. Needs to go her own way. She can't wait for me. Be on her own and become like whoever. Get away from here, get away from herself.

And me? Do I've go too, go it alone and then suffer for being lonely? Can't I do what the boys are doing? What does it matter? I wanted to avoid it all, but what if I can't, what if I just roll over into other problems. I can be someone else. I can be loads of things, all at once. Whatever I want. I can do it all.

Maybe Aoife doesn't get into college. Maybe she repeats her Leaving. Maybe I don't leave for the job. Maybe we go back to school together, the same school and get on well.

Or go our separate ways and that feels alright too?

Either way, can't leave it like this.

The lights come on as I head outside. Sweaty sighs and protests. The music's gone and the silence is a mental fucken banshee fucken shrieking in my ears.

I take out my phone. Click down through old messages. All from her, from ages ago. The whole thing mapped from first to last. But no room for no more to come through.

It's okay now I get it. I do. I delete all the old ones and make room for the new.

Give it a second and one comes through. Just the one, just from Barry. He's going home he says but the boys are in Brodericks. Not the boys he doesn't say the boys. They've all gone to Brodericks he says, that's where they are. Of course they're all there. I'm going there too.

Damie Rynne pulls up next to me, low down in his Subaru. *How's things Liam baiy*. I nearly tell him *man hard luck on the race, well run and that,* but that's a Sports Day like ten years ago and I know then I'm out of my gourd.

He offers me a lift home, but no, gourd or no gourd, I know you don't get in a Subaru at two o'clock in the morning. I'm not scared but I'm not stupid either. Anyway, I know where I'm going. Brodericks isn't far. He revs up, silver alloys, back tyres losing grip, left and right, before he screeches up away.

It's Enny's brother on the door of Brodericks so he lets me in even though it's past closing. They're still serving, just, cans of beer and cider. The apples sugar on my tongue in the gap between my lips and teeth. I know where I am.

I'm not sure the right thing to say, but I bet I think of something. I feel good. I must be good.

Ah look. There's Dave. There's Pa. There's Lisa. There's Enny. There's Aidan. There's Eimear. There's Spancil. There's Conor. There's Orla. There's Seánie, Séamie, Sharon.

There's Cusack.

There's Aoife.

He realises Aoife and CUSACK *are together.*

Oh.

Ha.

Ah that's criminal.

ACT THREE

PA *alone, lying down as at the beginning. Everything is dark, bar the streetlight as before and the flame from a lighter he's flicking on and off.*

CUSACK *enters, soaked from rain. He has come up fully now, likes being in the space, in his skin. He grabs a towel from* PA*'s hung-up clothes, smells it for damp, and dries his hair, etc. Then he lies down next to* PA. *Let them be for a moment. Then:*

CUSACK. You're still here.

PA. Ah.

CUSACK. That's good.

Where's Barry?

PA. Dunno.

CUSACK. Surprised he left.

PA. How far'd'you get?

CUSACK. End of the road there.

I was all set to go. Get home, see Aoife. Ask her why or what she sees in me; what are we doing. Ask the baby why he crawled, or her father if, whatever, is there any way out of all this. Was going to ask all of that. But I needed a shit.

PA. Ya?

CUSACK. Hopped the wall, took a shit. It felt good. Really. I understood why the baby's always smiling.

I realised too I was *fucked*.

PA. Sorry.

CUSACK. No.

PA. I didn't know you'd freak. I thought it was a normal amount.

CUSACK. No, no, I mean, I realised I'd come out tonight to get wrecked. Like I've been looking forward to this for weeks. Not this, exactly, but ya, getting fucked. Complaining I was bored and tired, desperate to get off my face.

And here I am.

PA. Here you are.

CUSACK. I get here and all I want is to go home to my family.

My family.

PA. Why din't you?

CUSACK. Cos I'm completely fucked! See? I did what I meant to do. No sense not enjoying it.

And when I get back later, in the morning or whatever, I'll know that that's where I wanted to be.

Beat.

PA. What'd'you use for toilet paper?

CUSACK. Wet wipes. I've shit loads of'm.

How long does this stuff last?

PA. Dunno. Couple more hours. You'll be grand in the morning.

CUSACK. Back to normal.

PA. Ya.

CUSACK. Will you talk to Séamie?

PA. Fuck him. It's a shithole. I'm too good for the place.

CUSACK. Where'll you go?

PA. – .

Shrugs.

Limerick.

CUSACK. Limerick?

PA. Ya.

CUSACK. That's not Ennis.

PA. These drugs have you fierce sharp.

CUSACK. D'you know anyone in Limerick?

PA. Where d'you think I got the stuff.

I'll be grand…

CUSACK. Have you ever lived outside Ennis?

PA. 'Lived'. I'n crashing on a couch, not fucken emigrating.

CUSACK. – .

You heading down tonight?

PA. No. I've to organise a few things. Sign on next week then I'll have money for the bus.

CUSACK. I could lend it to you.

PA. I wouldn't pay you back.

CUSACK. I don't mind.

PA. It's grand. I'd still need to come back to sign on. I'n not leaving it to them.

CUSACK. What about the Tesco thing?

PA. Stacking shelves?

CUSACK. It's a job.

PA. Exactly.

I dunno.

Sure my reference is gone now.

CUSACK. Have you the form there?

PA *takes the form from an inside pocket, gives it to* CUSACK. CUSACK *gets a pen and writes on the form. Gives it back.*

Now, when they ring to check up on you. Who'll answer?

(*Does a voice.*) 'This is Séamus. Ah ya. Model employee.'

PA. Tenant.

CUSACK. 'Ever'thing sure. No better man.'

(*Normal voice*.) Could be true.

Give's your lighter there.

PA. Have you fags?

CUSACK. No. Show's though.

PA *gives* CUSACK *the lighter.* CUSACK *gets up to light the candles.*

PA. Don't.

CUSACK. I fucken will.

He lights all the candles. As he does.

Longer they're lit, slower tomorrow comes.

Space is brighter now and flickering alive. CUSACK *gives* PA *back the lighter.*

Tomorrow. What day's tomorrow?

PA. Saturday.

CUSACK. Was it then too?

PA. Ya.

Last Friday before the Leaving. He was meant to move up on the Saturday.

CUSACK. Funny it fell again on a Friday.

PA. It didn't make people come out though did it?

Some years it was a Tuesday, a Wednesday, we still got a crowd. Even last year Thursday was better than this.

CUSACK. Cos I wasn't here?

PA. I thought this year, we'll do it right. Seventeen years ago. He was seventeen.

CUSACK. Ya.

PA. Do it properly, on the Friday. And this is fucken it.

CUSACK. What'll you do tonight?

PA. I dunno. I was hoping to stall here a few days till I got sorted but Barry was a prick and wouldn't give me the keys.

CUSACK. When do you sign on?

PA. Tuesday.

CUSACK. Three nights.

PA. We'll see sure. It's only tonight yet.

CUSACK. Always. Who's in Limerick?

PA. I know loads down there.

CUSACK. Ya but who?

PA. You wouldn't know'm.

CUSACK. Are they going to look after you?

PA. Dunno. Are you?

CUSACK. – .

PA. Ya. Be grand.

CUSACK. I used to be so jealous of you.

PA. What?

CUSACK. First few years. Apprenticing and after. I thought Aoife was going to dump me. She was down in Cork studying. I'd only see her when she came home to see her parents.

It was shit. Especially that first year. She was [depressed]. It was hard.

And she'd come home and we'd go out. And we'd see you. And ya I thought you were a waster not to be working.

PA. Sound.

CUSACK. There was me. Eighteen on a sixty-hour week. Texting her all night. Helping her through. Trying. I thought I had to stay awake every hour, fucken pulling at everything every fucken minute just to hold it all together.

And you. I thought. You didn't need anything.

PA. Now what d'you think?

CUSACK. Now I don't have time to think.

PA. Ha.

CUSACK. Hasn't changed that much. Sixteen, seventeen years. She's better usually. We added the kid.

I think you get old either way. And it's hard either way. Hard to keep what you have and hard to have nothing.

Liam got away with it.

PA. D'you think?

CUSACK. Definitely man. Seventeen? Got out at his peak. No recession.

PA. Didn't get fat.

CUSACK. Or go bald.

PA. You're the only one going bald.

CUSACK. Had that fucken stupid teenage love. Thought it meant everything but cost nothing in the long run.

PA. For Aoife.

CUSACK. For whoever. Fucken Santa Claus. He never found out it was nothing. Not nothing. But hard too.

D'you think it was?

PA. What?

CUSACK. – . What Barry said.

PA. I don't think Barry knew him as well as you or me or Aoife.

CUSACK. No.

That's not an answer either.

Remember what Rynne said?

PA. Fuck Rynne.

CUSACK. He said Liam was flat out in the middle of the road.

PA. Lying to dodge jail just.

CUSACK. If he was making it up, wouldn't he say he ran out in front of him or just got clipped?

Lying flat in the road?

PA. Lying through his teeth.

Aoife never comes.

CUSACK. Don't do that.

PA. Is that why?

CUSACK. They were finished.

PA. Just about.

CUSACK. Ages before. She told me.

Anyway. We were kids. Who remembers all that stuff?

PA. I do.

CUSACK. If he hadn't'a died would it bother us? It's childhood. You're meant to forget the details so you can look back and pretend it was great.

PA. It wasn't great.

CUSACK. And even if he was pissed off at Aoife and me? That's not our fault. That's a stupid reason. You don't lie down and die cos you once quite liked a girl.

PA. So what? Forget it?

CUSACK. Man. I know loadsa people who've topped themselves since. Lads on my course; nurses in with Aoife; developers; travellers. Short of the hurling it's the national fucken pastime.

We only remember Liam. What about them?

PA. I didn't know them.

CUSACK. I did. But I couldn't give a shit. Not really. Same thing every time. Families saying they were happy. Friends all surprised.

Everyone's happy till they're not.

Whatever. I'm happy. I'm thirsty. But I'm happy.

CUSACK *drinks*.

PA. How's the kid?

CUSACK. He's good. He's crawling.

PA. I heard. What's his name?

CUSACK. Pa.

PA (*surprised*). Is it?

CUSACK. No. It's Frankie.

PA. Prick!

CUSACK (*laughing*). Can you actually imagine [us naming our baby after you]?

(*Shaking head.*) Frankie though? Sake.

Will you never want all that?

PA. I dunno.

Is it good?

CUSACK. It's alright.

PA. Ya. Sure.

How're you feeling?

CUSACK. Good, ya. Have you more?

PA. A bit.

CUSACK *takes another bump off* PA. *It's casual and nice.*

BARRY *enters consternated.*

BARRY. Jesus Christ.

CUSACK. Barry, is that you?

You've been gone a while. Where were you?

BARRY. Where was I? I was looking for you.

CUSACK. I'm here.

BARRY. Check your phone.

CUSACK. Seventeen missed calls.

Now.

BARRY. I'm after traipsing through every pub in town looking for you. No one's around. Town's dead.

CUSACK. I was here.

BARRY. Sake.

CUSACK. I'm sorry. Like, I'm high, d'y'know?

PA. No one in Brodericks?

BARRY. No one. Bouncer wan't going to let me in even.

PA. Who was on?

BARRY. I didn't know him. Place was rammed. Crawling with kids.

CUSACK. Do they not have exams?

BARRY. I had to shout down to Dermot behind the bar. Only person I knew. The lads were kicked out apparently.

CUSACK. What happened?

BARRY. Enny getting thick. Some young fella wouldn't give him a fag.

CUSACK. 'Enny fags there?'

BARRY. Kid didn't smoke, but Enny wouldn't leave it. Tried to hit him.

PA. He boxed a kid?

BARRY. Tried to. Missed. Fell on his hole, split his head off the footrail. Dunno did he go home or to the hospital.

CUSACK. He has that ear infection as well. Been off all week. He shouldn't be out really, but sure.

BARRY. The rest just called it a night.

PA. No house party?

BARRY. Nothing. Aidan and Louise are away for the weekend, so they called it early. I got Dave on the phone. He was already in bed.

PA. Sake.

CUSACK. Just us three then.

BARRY. Just us.

D'ye want a drink?

CUSACK. No. Sit down

BARRY. I dunno. I'm all.

CUSACK. Come on. Come here.

BARRY *sits with the other two.*

BARRY. I knew no one. Twelve o'clock on a Friday night. Dermot, just, congratulating me on London.

CUSACK. That's nice.

BARRY. He was pulling the piss.

CUSACK. Really?

BARRY. Maybe. I dunno.

CUSACK. Are you comfy there?

BARRY. I am actually.

I'm wrecked.

I don't want to go home.

CUSACK *hugs* BARRY.

I like it here.

CUSACK. Ya.

PA. Ah.

BARRY. About twenty flights leave Shannon every day. Around four-thousand seats. Usually fairly full. So in an eight-hour shift I help around three thousand people leave. Watch'm go. Up and.

I can't even drive a car.

I don't know her. Not really. Didn't even know she *used* to go out with him, let alone...

Never thought she'd do something like this.

Eleven years.

How can I start again?

Find someone else to – love… who'll love me…

Find another flatmate even, fuck.

Thirty-fucken-four.

CUSACK. Ah.

BARRY. I was gone. If people hear I'm stayin.

CUSACK. No one will blame you.

BARRY. Do you think?

CUSACK. If you wanted to stay.

BARRY. You thought I should go.

CUSACK. Ya but. Now this.

BARRY. You knew about this. You still thought I should.

CUSACK. But now you know. It's different.

    You'll be alright.

BARRY. Back to work. Back home.

CUSACK. You'll still have us.

PA. No he won't.

CUSACK. Ah Pa of course he will.

PA. No. You're never out. I might be gone.

BARRY. Gone? Where?

PA. Limerick.

BARRY. What about Tesco?

PA. Sure why would they hire me? Experience and.

    I mean, what kind of experience. Stacking shelves? I mightn't
    even get it. Imagine going for it and not getting it?

    If I did, I mightn't take it.

CUSACK. Take it if you get it. Talk to Séamie. Stay in town.

(*To* BARRY.) You too.

BARRY. How?

CUSACK. People moving back now. Jobs and.

(*Settling down, dreamily.*) Be class. The lads again. We can do whatever. I really feel like this is our time coming.

PA. That's cos you're on drugs.

CUSACK. No, seriously.

– .

Maybe.

PA (*to* BARRY). You should go.

BARRY. How can I now?

PA. Go with her.

BARRY. She might not let me.

PA. Go without her so. Go on your own. Go anywhere. Cos this? [Is bullshit.]

CUSACK. 'S'nice though.

PA. My hole's nice.

People who were here.

BARRY. When?

PA. The night.

BARRY. Oh.

PA. Time, time.

BARRY. Ahhh…

CUSACK. Enny.

BARRY. Dave.

PA. Mark.

CUSACK. Lisa.

BARRY. Me.

PA. Conor.

CUSACK. Me.

BARRY. Séamie.

PA. Staples.

CUSACK. Aoife.

BARRY. Marita.

PA. Me.

CUSACK. Spancil.

BARRY. Seánie.

PA. D'anyone say Liam?

CUSACK. No.

PA. Liam.

BARRY. Liam wasn't here.

PA. What?

CUSACK. You have to drink.

PA. Course he was here. That's why we come here.

BARRY. No man. There were loads of us out playing darts that
    night, but not Liam.

PA. What are you talking about?

BARRY. He had his work thing remember? The lads from the
    kitchen?

    Remember, we went into town to meet him, but there was no
    sign. We walked in groups of two all along the old main road.
    Trying to hitch. It was me and Cusack, Enny and Spancil.

CUSACK. Ya.

PA. Me and Liam.

BARRY. No. He was with the kitchen fellas, yerman of the
    Mongans, few others maybe. We couldn't swing a lift.

CUSACK. I shoulda flashed a bit a' leg.

BARRY. So by the time we got into town I was wrecked. Everyone went to Brodericks but I was so pissed off from walking I just wanted to head home.

I was walking down the market, past Gracey's. Remember Gracey's? Where the bookies is now. And as I walked past I saw Liam inside. Off his face. I tried to get in but the bouncer ID'd me so I shouted in. Liam didn't hear me. Whatever. I sent him a text, let him know where ye were.

It's the last time I saw him. Bullshit. A nothing moment.

But he wasn't here.

PA. Then why do we come here?

BARRY. Cos we used to come here.

CUSACK. Just not that night?

BARRY. *We* were. But not Toner. He was gone. He was leaving.

PA. It definitely happened on the road out from here.

BARRY. *To* here, I think? Mighta been trying to sleep it off. Didn't want to go home drunk or whatever. Got sidetracked.

PA. No, I.

I thought he was here.

BARRY. Not with us.

PA. No?

Fuck.

I can't remember.

I can't.

CUSACK (*sensitive*). Let's play.

BARRY. We need drink.

CUSACK *rises, goes to the back for cans.* PA *and* BARRY *alone.*

PA. I loved him.

BARRY. Ya.

PA. Or.

No, but.

And not even.

I didn't even see him on his last fucken day.

BARRY. Ya.

PA. Why are we still here man?

BARRY. Cos nowhere else is open.

BARRY kisses PA on the top of the head as he stands.

Here, can you do me a favour. I'm not going to have time to drop these back.

BARRY gives PA the keys to the place.

Ya?

PA. Ya.

CUSACK comes back carrying as many cans as he can. Playing a video on his phone.

CUSACK. See him there.

The other two look at the phone screen. It's a moment.

PA. He doesn't get far does he?

CUSACK. No. He has his father's arse poor fucker.

Something happens in the video. They laugh.

BARRY. Class.

CUSACK. Be twice as hard to keep up with him now, by fuck.

Anyway.

Puts away his phone.

Cans to see who goes first?

PA. There's no advantage going first.

BARRY. But there's every advantage in a can.

The three skull cans. BARRY gives up first. Then CUSACK. This is second nature to PA.

CUSACK. Brgh. Pa's first.

They begin to play the game. It goes normally at first. The director is free to determine how the game plays out within the rules, but, broadly, PA is best; CUSACK is annoyed that the drugs are interfering with his aim and throw, and BARRY is the average of the other two.

There'll be some jockeying of position, and some dispute over where e.g. BARRY's dart was placed (from CUSACK, likely, as he is losing), but the game will go smoothly, each playing to win, insofar as they're able, with PA out in front.

About halfway through, BARRY's phone begins to ring.

Leave it.

BARRY (*checking*). It's Róisín.

PA. Take your go.

BARRY. D'you think…?

CUSACK. Leave it man.

PA. Play.

They go back playing.

BARRY *has more force in his throws now. Swears when he misses.*

PA *starts to throw badly now. Hits a twenty, drinks for twenty. Hits another twenty, drinks for even longer.*

On his third go, PA *misses the board.*

CUSACK. That's a minute!

PA *drinks for a minute, or more.*

Jaysus.

Maybe a moment of overweening flourish from CUSACK.

Then, on his next three goes, PA *throws three bullseyes, meaning the other two have to drink for a minute each, each time.*

Oh fuck.

BARRY. Jesus Pa.

CUSACK. Oh fuck. I quit.

CUSACK *goes to the toilet to vomit.*

BARRY. Fucken hell.

BARRY *isn't feeling the best.*

You win.

Jesus.

PA. I always win.

BARRY (*walks towards toilet, taking out phone*). You were always the best. (*Listening to voicemail.*)

PA. Always will be.

What she say?

BARRY. Said she was just calling me back. Said she couldn't make out my message. Bad coverage. Said she'd see me when I get home.

PA. That's lucky.

BARRY. I suppose.

PA. You can do whatever you want now.

BARRY. Ya.

Long beat, as this lands.

CUSACK *comes back, cleaning his mouth with a wet-wipe.*

CUSACK. So that toilet doesn't flush.

What are we at now?

BARRY. Walking.

CUSACK. Ya?

BARRY. Ya.

CUSACK. Can I come?

BARRY. Pa?

PA. I dunno.

CUSACK. Why? Fuck the two of ye.

BARRY. Tell him.

PA. Nah.

BARRY. Do. (*To* CUSACK.) You know Rynne?

CUSACK (*grave*). Ya.

BARRY. You know he didn't get prosecuted?

CUSACK. He lost his licence though.

BARRY. He nearly lost his licence. But they let him keep it cos the new road divided his farm. If he couldn't drive he said, he couldn't look after his cattle.

CUSACK. Really?

BARRY (*to* PA). Tell him.

PA. – .

The first year after, I went out to Rynne's. I wanted him to come down so I could kill him. I was emotional. But he wouldn't.

So I went walking. Across the bypass. Out to the other side of his farm, where he'd moved his cowshed to. A fifteen-minute drive in the tractor. A ten-minute walk from his door.

Cows are just stupid. Or sound or whatever. I opened the door and let them out. Spent an hour or two chasing a few of them away from the herd. Off across different fields.

Then I went back and slashed his tyres.

I like to do it every year. Tradition.

CUSACK. Seriously?

PA. But it's too late now. It's nearly bright.

BARRY. It's not.

PA. It's better done in the dark.

BARRY. Please man.

We've time still. Just about.

PA. We'd be seen.

CUSACK. Three of us? Nah. We'd be three times quicker.

Plus them clouds. Be night for a while yet.

BARRY. Exactly.

PA. D'you reckon?

CUSACK. Definitely man.

BARRY. Yes!

Pa?

PA. – .

Ya.

BARRY. Hmon so.

CUSACK. Savage.

CUSACK *rushes off.*

BARRY. Blow out those candles.

PA *starts blowing out candles.*

CUSACK *comes back armed with cans.*

CUSACK. Few tins.

BARRY. Sure baiys.

CUSACK. I'n not ready to be sober yet.

BARRY. Ya. (*To* PA.) You ready?

PA. Ah.

CUSACK *and* BARRY *exit as* PA *blows out the second last candle.*

*

Liam Part III – spoken by PA (holding one last candle)

There are basically two ways to throw a dart; the easy way, the obvious one, you keep the point up and the flights down and it kinda lobs its way into the island but the harder way, the better way, you keep the point down and the flights up so it dips and fucken flies dead straight. The harder way is better cos if you get it you're not blocking your next darts with the flights of the first one.

That's high-end stuff though, expertise shit; probly only matters when you're class or really class. Two ways whatever to throw a dart but they're all heading for the same thing at the end of the day.

I think for a second that's deep but maybe it's just good to know how to be good at something.

I'm walking away now from town, feeling cold, feeling brisk. Wanna walk fast, get there, get to Pointers, but I'm having to mind my step. At night the stones and the grass all look the same. Need my feet to see for me. Feeling out the push of rock, the give of grass.

If I get to Pointers I'll know where I am.

The Rocky Road. Town's traffic in the distance. Fifty quid to the taxi-man if you puke in the back of the cab. Can't afford that, have a nice little puke in the bushes cos I've manners.

Walking's nice though, rush of blood. I cross the grass and see beyond the cleared-out land for the bypass. A thousand streetlamps not turned on yet. When does it open?

A year from now the new job's good. Like, it's hard, but it *is* good. I can feel the heat of the gantry lights on the back of my hand as I serve. We're plating up soufflés. Two hundred; Jesus. A presidential visit. Chef is happy. Aoife's coming up at the weekend. She's going to transfer courses.

One of the soufflés starts to collapse. Bin it, lads, we've time.

That's not yet. I'm here now, back on the Rocky.

The Rocky Road's not really a road, it's like a track, but it's fucken old, like older'n Ennis. Ancient farmers driving cattle from the outskirts of a village to the outskirts of a town.

Desire paths she says they're called when we walk that day to Pointers. Whose desire? Herding nervous livestock, tramping ground until it's barren. Ruts to show our habits. Nothing grows where we always go.

They open this university and at first they don't build paths between the buildings. After a year they find brown trails. Pave over what feet laid.

New York's a grid. 'Magine the wind. I can feel it.

The streets in town are formed by monks studying at the Abbey. Build their huts, year on year, prayer and devotion night and day, till the grass blanches and stops growing. Now it's shops and pubs where people work all day and night.

We walk the path of our desire. She desires me then and I desire her, but now there's no way back between us.

If there are other places Pa reckons there are other times too. Where things that never happen here happen there, and things that happen here never ever happen there.

I'm planting saplings in the garden on the morning of my thirtieth. They'll grow in time and so will our baby. By the time he's ten we can build him a treehouse.

Or I'm up in university taking a shortcut across the res. Smoking a pinner in the sun. I'm sleeping with a girl I meet in the Yoga Society. She's tutoring me in my feminist elective, what? I keep in touch with Aoife and it's nice that we're still friends.

Or we stay together forever and we both clean up our act.

I've no drugs or drink now. Not on me, but still in me. I'm very fucked. Fuck you very much. Hear cars and lorries on some road somewhere. Not here cos the new road's not finished. See streetlamps in the distance, clear lines of orange. High-waisted skirts of light, darkness in between.

I go to America on a J1 visa. We buy an old jalopy and drive from New York to San Diego. We run out of gas and have to push the car through miles of desert, sand and stone scraping into the dry grit of the engine. We get stuck outside Death Valley and stare up at stars.

Constellations are shit though. Even with the lines joined up, I don't see twins, or a bird.

Except the Plough obviously. I think someone one day sees the Plough and says look a plough and everyone's like, yeah, good call, and then he gets cocky. Look, a bull. A bull?

Just because you can see two things doesn't mean there's a path between'm. You have to make it over. Maybe it goes nowhere, like the Rocky. Alright, go back, start again.

Frankie says you can tell the Rocky's useless by the fact there's a campaign to save it. If anyone actually needed it, it'd be used and then repaired. People'd be protesting for *more* roadworks, politicians'd be doing interviews standing next to potholes. The old main road was a track once too, but no one's worried about that. It's all nature, old and new, he says. Just some of it we use and the rest we ignore.

If we needed it he goes we wouldn't ignore it.

Still it's weird to see the ground gouged through – diggers blocking the path. One still has the headlights on – white beams punching out like arms. Beyond it the green of the grass reflects white, pointing to the start of the site. That's the new road.

Normally takes like five, ten minutes to get to Pointers; turn right off the main road, totter over the slugga, past the new estate, the cave and the weird quarry bit. After that it's the tree and the spot where she, where me and her, where we kiss… but then it's the stream, and the gate and I'm there. But I'm past the gate here and the stream's just there so…

First time we come here, man, it's the worst. Cusack's giving Pa shit, Barry's up ahead cos he hates a row.

That weed plant. Me thinking I'm finished.

I tell Mam it's Pa's and she believes me. Pa doesn't complain. Says he knows this place out the Rocky, and keeps the facts between me and him. Even when the lads give out. Why don't I say anything? Embarrassing. We arrive at the place, thinking we're finished then thinking we're saved.

A run-down shack. A hut with a dartboard. It's shit, like, but we love it, name it. Bringing people out to *Pointers*. (*Fondly.*) Stupid name. The boys even have their party there tonight. But then they don't stay, they come into town instead to hit the pubs, and. And when they leave for college? What'll happen then?

I know Pa my whole life. And just like that he takes it. They blame him forever. He never says a word.

The way out of one thing becomes another sticking rut.

I'm climbing up the digger now, to see what I can see. The beam is pointing downwards. Facing west I guess. An early dawn must be behind me.

The new road's cutting north to south. Pointers I *know* is south. I could always head that way. It might be quicker.

It's our twenty-year reunion and me and Pa are smoking a doob out the back of the school. He can't handle it, lightweight baiy. We're idiots but it's nice. There's a dinner afterwards. Our partners get on well.

You can do whatever you want. And we do. Barry's a painter or an architect. Pa's a millionaire. Cusack's still a cunt, but he's sound now too. We do it all.

Cos it's funny. There are so many things to do. To see and smell and hear. To take and use and drink. But that's not what they mean.

They mean: get a course, get a job, get a house. So much promise. We can do whatever we want. Choose any number of ways to get to that one place.

Parents listing adventures they wish that they. Instead a' double-dip recessions. Emigration, dole. That never happens again.

We always have it easy. It never goes wrong for us.

One day the cars come here, haring past the town, right past us, knowing nothing about us. Everyone saying it's great. One day. A great way to get away.

Speeding cos we're late for the ceremony. I'm Pa's best man, speech in my pocket. They make a lovely couple. I say I can't believe he's found someone to put up with him. Aoife says I can't say that, but I do, obviously. At least the baby's calm. Hope it lasts. I gun the engine, it roars richly. We won't be late.

I'm coming down the far side of the peak. Dry tongue, jaw aches. The hill brows and the crispness has run from the edges of things. Lines have softened. I blink and it's dawn.

Can I do this forever? Do I want to? Whatever I want.

The tarmac's smooth and even slippy. Light rain, slick, like almost soft. Lanes not yet marked. Broad as fuck. Goes on forever.

Tomorrow's now today. A few hours till I pack and go. Dad's driving me up. Tonight my first shift starts.

A couple quick games of darts. That's all. Or just walking. Light a candle. Watch the light.

Half the sky is bright above, stars still in the rest. The noise of traffic over, some louder, near. East there. West.

Underneath no push of rock, no give of grass. It's all new now, no room for any old. Paving over. This isn't the first time I've been right here I'd say but I don't recognise it cos it's never been now before.

Sit down the ground is damp. My head is heavy on my neck. Lie down it's kinda cool. Gaps in the surface, my face filling'm in. It's cold and then it's warm. The bone of my brow tender against the road.

All the things that I could do. All the ways it could turn out.

We get what we want and make only good choices and no one learns an'thing the hard way. We work hard in school and we're kind to our mothers; we get savage fucken jobs and buy our own houses; we remember our friends and get together every year and the world just gets better and better forever.

Headlights beam over the brow of the road. Is that here?

When we look at the horizon, does the light curve, or are we looking at a tangent?

The sound bends. The boy-racers. Empty road pure class joyriding. Subarus skidding, doughnutting rain. Is that now?

If the world were flat we'd see everything coming and everything that's gone before.

Gravel rattles the underside of the engine.

I'm walking through the desert, my face on the macadam. She holds onto my hand as we're running to the church.

Some of this is now, all of it could be.

Damie Rynne is now alright. Can I see him? Look at him there, pulling the wheel, pure sliding.

Can I see him? From *here*?

Can he see me?

I think I've time. To roll, have I? Maybe move, out of the way, alright, I think I can, I think, can I?

Which way does he go? And which way then do I?

Or I go first and he goes after.

One before the other. But everything is and happens altogether. For once and for all.

Oh.

Ha.

Ya.

The dawn blinks.

End.

SINK

For one actor

Author's Note

The Boys' School in Smock Alley Theatre, Dublin, is an atmospheric space for a play. Two church windows sit high and asymmetrically on the back wall of the stage, a wall built out of small red bricks that are chipped and crumbling with age. Audiences filter in from behind this wall and down around a sloping ramp to take their seats in church pews, waiting in semi-darkness for the show to begin.

In the first production the director, Thomas Martin, had set the performer, Rachel Feeney, on stage before the audience entered. Poised atop a plinth, Rachel would lie against the back wall as though the wall were the ground and the audience were watching over her. She waited there, ghostly, in that kind of repose that looks like it could be sleep or death, until the lights shifted and the play began.

For an hour or so it was the only repose she got; *Sink* is a demanding prospect for an actor, with its mix of language and storytelling styles, and it was astonishing to watch Rachel emobdy Ciara and Bríd alternately, giving distinct, discrete postures, voices and personalities to them both.

The decision that the play should be delivered by a single performer alone is meant to highlight the doubling and cyclical action that defines the play, not only in overlapping themes and the interplay of coincidence, but in the storylines the protagonists follow: both women travel west from a tense and overbearing city to the apparent peace of the countryside only to be harassed and disconcerted by the recurrence of traumatic memories from their childhoods. Both seek to move past the anxiety these memories provoke – Ciara by trying to bring what's unconscious to consciousness, Bríd by trying to repress and forget – and both women ultimately find a higher purpose in sacrificing their self-preservation for the salvation of another: Bríd shields a little girl from a traumatic experience of her own, Ciara fails to recall her own trauma but rescues an old man from alcoholic self-destruction.

Ciara and Bríd have opposing beliefs when it comes to memory, but they both come to an uneasy truce with their respective pasts, recognising that the ordinary business of living is a painful mystery – it was ever thus, and maybe no amount of self-excavation can change that.

I first started thinking about the ideas that would become *Sink* in the summer of 2018 when a heatwave struck Ireland and a host of archaeological finds were discovered as land dried out and outlines of henges, enclosures and other tombs were made visible in the scorched earth. It got me thinking about climate change and how it related to our past, and it struck me that many of the bog bodies that have been found in Ireland were probably, as Ciara says in the play, 'Ritual sacrifice: tribal leaders probably, killed by their own people and buried. A punishment for bad weather, or an offering for better harvests.'

That seemed to me to be an exact doubling of what's happening nowadays – people being so fearful of their future, so terrified of what their climate would do to them, that they would risk self-destruction and violence against their institutions of authority in the hope that peace might be delivered in the aftermath.

We're living now with the mistakes that previous generations made; our traumas – of climate, of economy, of personality even – happen and recur because of how our immediate ancestors shaped the world to suit their short-term needs. And the world that the next generation gets to live in will be shaped entirely by our success or failure today to correct the errors of those generations that went before us.

If we are able to safeguard that future, it will be because the old modes of living have finally run dry. The choices we make now cannot just be the same old choices, and they cannot be choices just for us. We're living cloaked in the remains of the past, but we need to start thinking in full awareness of the future – it is our capacity for imagining ourselves across time, perhaps disregarding the past, certainly protending the future, that will determine whether our descendants sink or swim.

That feeling, of living across time, of channelling trauma and playing host to other people's pain, of sacrificing yourself and accepting the irresolvability of the mysterious way the past recurs is what drove the writing of *Sink*. Love and empathy are key – the idea that we might give up our own desires for the needs of others is the communality that can shape a friendship, a relationship, a family or a tribe. It is not the individual but the collective that gets prioritised. It is a calculated risk – it is not the burning of others to save ourselves, but the offering of oneself to save another – that might allow us all to survive.

Each night on stage Rachel had to pick apart these offerings, these knotty, interwoven thoughts delivered in two distinct modes of language – one discursive, one reflexive; one conversational, one pre-conscious – and tell a story that crossed multiple characters in a single setting across multiple timelines. For an hour. And audiences had to dig deep too, pull apart the story strands and find what was buried in the language.

It was never not a big ask, but hopefully what was waiting to be discovered was a sense of hope, an idea that we are often where we always were, but we also always have the opportunity to change, to give ourselves up and break the cycles that confine us. Whether those cycles are made up of the oppression of personal traumatic memory, or the damage done by the systems we live in – as is the case in both *Sink* and *Flights* – the answer is always in looking outside ourselves and offering up what we each might need from one another.

John O'Donovan
January 2020

Sink was first performed at the Boys' School, Smock Alley Theatre, Dublin, on 10 September 2019, in a One Duck production, as part of the Dublin Fringe Festival, with the following cast and creative team:

CIARA/BRÍD   Rachel Feeney

Director   Thomas Martin
Sound   Jon McLeod
Lighting   Cillian McNamara
Costume   Susan Yanofsky
Set   Dermot McMahon
Stage Manager Georgia Piano
Producers   Alan Mahon
                John O'Donovan

104

Acknowledgements

Thanks are due to Ailbhe Hogan, Alan Mahon, Tom Martin,
Amy Bunce, Brad Birch, Brian Cullinan, Deirdre O'Halloran
and the Bush Theatre, Michelle Fox, Dermot and Rachel
McMahon, the Mill Theatre Dundrum, Bee Sparks and all the
staff at Dublin Fringe for their invaluable contributions to the
development of the play and production.

Sink couldn't have happened without the generous support of people who donated to its fundraising campaign, so I'd like to thank Michael Abubakar, Derek Anderson, Matt Applewhite, Sam Bailey, Melissa Barry, Sonali Bhattacharyya, Brad Birch, Adam Brace, Maurice Brooks, Amy Bunce, David Byrne, John Callinan, Martina Callinan, Callum Cameron, Emily Collins, Mark Conway, Jude Cook, Frances Cooke, Nicola Coughlan, Rebecca Crookshank, Brian Cullinan, Georgia De Grey, Kieran Dee, Michael Dee, Ronan Dennehy, Sean Denyer, Ammar Duffus, Janin Eberhardt, Mike Farquhar, Sarah Foster, Flavia Frasier-Cannon, Niven Govinden, Afsaneh Gray, Jodi Gray, Gillian Greer, Aoife Guilfoyle, Fidelma Hanrahan, Sadie Hasler, Ciara Hassett, Damien Hasson, Maddie Hindes, Emily Hockley, Ailbhe Hogan, Dervla Hogan, Niall Hogan, Patrick Holt, James Huntrods, Sara Joyce, Dave Keenan, Fergus Kelly, Stephen Kelly, Arinzé Kene, Hannah Khalil, Matt Kibble, Sarah Kosar, Gabriele Lampis, Steve Laughton, Cethan Leahy, Morgan Lloyd Malcolm, Finbar Lynch, Ed MacLiam, Andrew Maddock, Amber Massie-Blomfield, Karen McCartney, Declan McMahon, Dermot McMahon, Rachel McMahon, David McMullin, Barry McStay, Aidan Murphy, Richard O'Brien, Rachel O'Byrne, Patrick O'Donnell, Vinay Patel, Margaret Perry, Danelle Pettman, Stewart Pringle, Paul Quinn, Marty Rea, Kathy Rucker, Matt Scott, Amal Shire, Emma Sinclair, Al Smith, Jessica Stewart, Will Storan, Eileen Walsh, Benjamin Weatherill, Tamara von Werthern, Sarah Liisa Wilkinson, Nathan Lucky Wood and Tom Wright, as well as our many kind and anonymous donors – it's always such a surprise and a delight that people are willing to back a play in its early stages – I'll be forever grateful to you all for your help in bringing *Sink* to the stage.

John O'Donovan

Characters

CIARA, *younger, from the city*
BRÍD, *older, from the country*
NEITHER/BOTH

Note

Bríd's lines should be delivered as often as possible in a single breath until the line-break. This won't always be possible, but aiming for that will help towards the rhythm.

Lines given in square brackets indicate words not said, but meant by gesture.

NEITHER/BOTH

Something's after happening

Something's always after

A grave fills up with water

A river runs low

The oceans rise, the fields dry out

Bones reappear; happens all over

But who does it happen to? You?

A shovel in soft ground severs the roots that hold the soil.
Bones are lowered covered. The roots repair and push through
bone like waves through water. The bones resurface. The world
takes notice.

Is this you noticing? You being noticed?

It has to start somewhere, even at the end.

But who should start it? And where?

CIARA

The office. Stinking heat.

Stuffed in a meeting room with no blinds. Sun everywhere.

I'd open a window, but outside's all traffic fumes.

We're all fanning ourselves. I can hear the sweat running down
the backs of people's knees.

Breathing in used breath by the litre. Mouths like exhaust pipes.

I can't wait for the weekend. Three days till. A break from the
city. And Mam has a garden.

Outside a city bus is buried in gridlock.

Hannah starts the slideshow. The projector roars in effort.

Images aren't great – portrait shots of landscape sites.

The odd aerial. Fancy fuckers with their drones.

We hop around sunburnt fields, dust burning on the lens.

Because of the drought, there's loads coming up.

So much, we're going out in ones. What?

We'll go wherever, check it out, if it's serious we get a team.
Ah fuck sake.

Hannah lists assignments, flicking slides.

Beside my window the bus window sweats.

That bus goes all the way to Mam's. Garden, tree and breeze.
Can't wait.

There's a girl on the bus, four or five. Red-faced, hot, hawing
on the glass.

Plastic little shades, cartoon fish. Gas like.

She gives me a wave, I give her a smile.

Hannah's droning on. Next slide.

Tannins, bogs, Dungiven?

I smile out at the girl again but her face has fallen asunder.

She's bawling. What?

She's looking at our screen.

I look up at what she sees. Oh [shite].

I look away at my files but see it there too.

Twisted bone. Grimaced flesh.

Human remains. That's serious.

I'm about to look at the girl again when Hannah asks do I agree.

(*Out.*) Sounds good.

I wasn't listening.

The bus drives off. Sorry...

Hannah goes next slide and I gather I'm going to Dungiven.

*

(*Her phone is in play.*)

Mam has me on speaker.

She's clearing out my old room so I can move back.

Wish she'd wait till I'm there.

But it makes sense. I hate the place I'm in; damp and airless, half my wages.

Be good for her too. Bit of company.

She hasn't been eating properly. Says she doesn't like cooking for one.

I said why don't I come over and cook?

She said why don't I come over and stay?

Why not? Going back doesn't mean going backwards.

I hear another bin bag ripping off the roll.

The days will tear away.

I should say something, cos if we have to dig, it'll mean delays and...

First I tell her about the little girl.

She doesn't hear me. Or.

She asks if I want to keep anything before she dumps it.

Maybe can she hold off till I'm there? I'd be happy to sort it all for her.

No, she'll get rid. If there was something I needed I'd a' had it by now.

I wouldn'ta just forgotten.

She might be dumping anything though.

Something goes in the bag. Close my eyes but I can't quite see.

The shelf. What's on it? The wardrobe…

(*Can't see.*)

I say again about the girl. Four or five, like. Probably never seen a body.

We mighta scarred her for life?

Mam's like nah – (*Dismissive, abrupt.*)

Everything washes over you at that age.

I try to say about the dig but the words slip down my throat.

Maybe don't say anything.

If it's nothing, I'll be back Friday.

I fold and unfold, pack and unpack, like will I say? D'I have to?

Another bag stacks. She's haring, happy, busy. I see her clearer there than I can see myself.

Happy.

Here's what I'll do, I'll pack here now and if I'm not back by Friday, we'll work something out.

Why worry her?

Shoulda done this years ago she goes.

I see her surrounded by bags. Buried. All that old all over I wonder what we're losing.

BRÍD

Please God I might soon sleep.

CIARA

Up half the night packing, then onto the bus like death-warmed-up.

We ooze out of the station and I get out my files.

Forms, statements, draft map of the site.

There's a tractor blocking traffic on the far side of the river. A tractor. Middle of town [?!].

The old woman beside me doesn't see. She doesn't look right actually, all mumbling.

I ask is she okay. No answer. Doesn't want to know. Fair enough.

I stick in my earbuds, get back to my file.

Clonycavan, Croghan, Cashel.

All recent-ish, found by turf-cutters.

That'll happen less now the bogs are decommissioned. They want to make them carbon neutral, or even carbon sinks.

If global warming stops, we'll find fewer finds. Get a future, forget the past.

Big 'if'.

(*Back to her files.*)

My body got found cos of the drought. Some walker stumbling in dried-out fields sees it squeezing its bones out to the surface.

The other bog bodies have been healthy – for corpses anyway. Young, mostly men, rich and well fed.

Country boys all bread and milk.

But their fatalities coincide with pre- and post-mortem injuries: axes to the face, lacerated nipples, nooses. Meaning?

Ritual sacrifice: tribal leaders probably, killed by their own people and buried. A punishment for bad weather, or an offering for better harvests.

The earth then acts as a seal: wet bog keeps out the oxygen; acid stops the rot.

Tannin turns them brown. Reddens the hair.

They knew what they were doing. Dying for their people.

If they were afraid, they kept going.

We have their stomach, their guts. Sometimes the bones dissolve, so you've to be careful excavating. What looks solid can fall asunder.

Is this the job? Putting shape on messy things. Teasing out truths from a handful of facts.

Could overthink all this for sure. So I do.

When I next look up, we're out of the city.

Fields and animals, happy sun. Ridiculous.

The old woman's asleep. Hand in her lap, skin slack on her bones. I could nearly touch her.

Nana lived back west. Mam's mam. The bus took hours.

I'd'a been itching to read. Mam'd'a been jabbering, nervous about Nana. We'd a' both probly fallen asleep.

BRÍD

Something's after happening start again start from the end

First rain since when no sleep but soon please God I might

Beyond the rain the lake the child the bottle the woman the bus the clinic

Starting from the end and ending from the start hang on have I gone wrong

CIARA

I wake in Limerick; shaking from the nap.

Files've slipped and stuck to the floor, reach over.

The old woman's gone. What?

There are stops before the station. She coulda hopped off.

But I didn't clock us stopping. Didn't feel her go.

Fucken relax. I shouldn'ta slept. I'm sweating, shook, and I've loads to do in Dungiven if I want to get back by Friday.

Change for the local bus. Try again with the files but.

Out the window's a little déjà vu; sun, animals, fields.

Wait though. Something's after happening. I know this road; that bridge; those houses.

The old woman's face comes back a second but no, not that, not her.

Before I've placed the feeling I see the sign.

Annadarmot.

We pull in at a petrol station, the driver goes 'Dungiven'.

Sorry, I say, where are we? Dungiven. The sign says Annadarmot. That's the old name she goes. They never changed the sign. But in Dungiven we are she says surely.

But Annadarmot. I mean – I *have* been here. Nana lived here.

*

We came here when Dad got bad and.

Mam was brilliant. Got us away.

It was cool at Nana's. I could talk out loud, play outside, leave books wherever.

At night I'd dream he'd follow us, but I'd wake and Mam'd be there. Happy.

Happy there.

In my head we stayed for ages but the sun was always shining, so it can't'a been long.

And we came after Nana died to sort the house.

Was that the same time or?

Was it even really here?

*

The sign's fucked, rust splitting the layers. The lettering's dull but it's there. Annadarmot.

Maps gives Dungiven; there I am, blue dot putting me in my place.

I nearly text Mam [but].

I just need to get this done so I can get back and move.

Find my B&B, survey the site, make a start.

BRÍD

Starting from the end no ending from the start please God I might soon sleep

Before that though the bus go back go home and start

Leaving the city after weeks dry-heaving it out of me not praying now practising sobriety

Repeat after me the doctor goes I go and I repeat

Walk House Pill Bottle Baby Save Salt Leave Calm Rain

Very good she goes improving so she ticks the file

These exercises are important to your short-term memory so but outside city-noise inside hospital-sound awake for weeks miles and miles and miles from home and

Go again Bríd please I start Walk but no she says start from the end so

Walk no oh am amamam Rain indeed so

Rain so Calm okay Leave ya Salt right Save lovely Baby getting there Bottle okay Pill House

Don't forget Walk she goes Walk not walking I'll take the bus

My head I'm gone the station bus the road back west my bed my own but she pulls me back and pulls in close and says you have to try

To rebuild short-term memory ya the only way you'll improve right

Korsakoff of course I can not dementia but close enough it means she says I need to eat nutrition and I need to sleep

Prescription here appointment there down home

Exercise your memory I will I said I won't forget

And dig deeper too No

Remember why you started please identify your triggers no now learn to cope without the drink no no no do you see

I'm away I'll say anything get away I say Okay

And come back if you've any trouble

No trouble worse than the trouble here no coming back I'm sticking to it dry forever no matter what not coming back

CIARA

Coming down Main Street, nothing.

No cars. No people.

The sun is high and hot and you can smell on the breeze that the river's low.

Pat Whelan, yerman who reported the find, said he'd meet me at the bridge at noon and bring me to the site.

There's the bridge, shimmering.

I'm trying to see if I remember, but I'm blanking.

Was it this quiet?

Motorway now means no traffic here but back then Main Street woulda been jammed. Exhausts and hot tar, not the tangy kinda pissy smell of the dried-out river.

There's the post office. Need to check the hours actually.

Sooner I get the paperwork to Hannah, sooner I get a team to relieve me. The sooner I'm back up with Mam.

Door's locked though. Windows dust heavy. Closed years.

Counter's shuttered – floor's littered with boxes for like Wham Bars and Refreshers and

Oh ya – fucken –

I'm sitting on the counter – on my own am I? Someone, Mam probly, buys me… something…

A Push Pop!

The ads like. Gas. They weren't cheap either. Thanks Mam!

Munching for ages, trying to bite to the spine.

I finish it and all. Reddened spit, sticky fist.

Love it. Simple pleasures. Eat a lolly, play in the sun.

Nobody worried about anything.

So much for the future, the village is dead now. Not even a post office like.

I see a man on the bridge – did he come up from the riverbank? He's walking away from me – limp on him but he's quick.

It's not yet noon.

MISTER WHELAN!

He kinda speeds up, does he?

MISTER WHELAN! IT'S CIARA, FROM –

Next thing, hand on my elbow. Frightens the shit a' me. This woman. Different woman. Not as old.

Says she's Pat Whelan.

Oh. Right. Sorry. I thought…

But he's gone.

*

We don't cross the bridge. She takes me down a track this side, across a field of rushes cracking as we walk.

Pat's chatty. Lives up-river. Always knew there was something.

The whole area's eerie, she reckons, laying it on thick.

(*Point these out*.) The river narrows to a ditch;

Abandoned-looking cottage;

Cars roaring on the motorway.

She's just above there.

Leave the cottage on your left, keep going, you can't miss her.

Right.

And here, she says, we're walking on a lake.

What?

Ten months out of twelve, this is a turlough. A lake that springs or drains like that – (*Snap on 'that'.*)

Common here. To do with the weather. They can dry up overnight then refill in an hour if the rain's heavy enough.

Right now it's bone. But once it rains and the river rises. That ditch'll rush like mad.

Makes sense so to bury here. If it's ritual.

Imagine. Thirsty people, terrified of drought.

With a heatwave where it's always rained.

You'd do anything to get the water back.

So do I think it's something? (*Pat's asking.*)

I nearly don't see it and when I do I realise I'm relieved.

I musta been scared it'd be a baby or a rake a' babies or.

It's an adult.

Bit on the small side.

Skeletal mostly, which is unusual. Maybe the saltwater…

Some flesh here and there.

His skull's face-down, decent head of hair.

Pat's excited. Visions of tourists. She looks the type to start a teashop.

It looks good, I say. And it does.

I'd love to start digging straight away. But I can't. Like, I'm not allowed.

We'll need to get a team alright.

I bend down close, take photos. Breathing in.

Smells of nothing first.

But then, it's –

Too-strong tea.

Coins.

The pissy low-tide.

I'd love to; but I shouldn't. So I don't.

I stand instead and get the forms for Pat.

No: I've left them at the B&B. Fuckit.

Draw the site map now, and post it off. That's the main thing.

Can I come up to her later with the forms?

Any time she says. Gives me the directions again. Cross, left, past the ditch, can't miss it.

I sketch out the site map and secure the remains with a tarp. I ask is there a risk of dogs or walkers?

But apparently no one walks here.

If no one walks here, how come she stumbled across him?

I sound like *CSI*.

But she starts chatting mindfulness and nature and I can't, this heat, I've way too much, I cut across and ask about post, she goes

BRÍD

Starting from the end the rain but now no rain for weeks can't sleep

This heat this dry can't hot dry nights

The thirst is worse drinking water fool my mouth then up and down coming out of me clear piss it into the cistern nearly 'steada wasting water

I try not to wake him he's up early to open he goes are you right there love I am I say I just can't sleep

He lands an arm across my chest to comfort but it weighs I say

I might get up and not be useless here but he stirs and says he'll get up too

No I go I'm grand I'll sleep so we lie there both him sleeping me lying till I'm at the counsellor answering questions

Little fan blowing hot air round your one there like

Did your father drink

Did your mother drink

Does your husband drink

What's your earliest memory a' drink

Have you any children drink

Have you any friends drink

Do you drink much drink

Would you drink if you drink

How drink is the drink you drink

I come away out and the sun is beating bearing down delivering thirst

Get it all clear if I could start from the end not going back all them questions end from the start

But the sun down on top of me was it ever so warm my throat so dry my lungs whistle tunes but I think of that clinic all them questions

I need to eat walk house and I need to sleep pill bottle

I go into the shop and buy a pint a pint of milk drink that instead

Walking home the heatwave baby the milk erupts comes up again so white and watery save and salt but I'm home and in leave and calm and out the heat I'm fine again

That night no sleep but nightmares still

Why did you start did your mother no no

What's your earliest memory no

Dig back deep start from the beginning no begin

I want I try to be better I try

My earliest memory

seven white communion dress

and five the garden Dadda dig the path

and four do I remember no and I don't know what's beyond that

the little girl at the end who who

Don't want to dig that path so deep no don't remember

And out he comes up out of bed his heavy hand you right
there love

And I am I say but I'm not I cry I don't know why

I cry I say I just can't sleep could I not have a small one cry just
a small one help me sleep

And he looks at me like I broke his heart but I swear it's just
to sleep

Maybe we should ring above the clinic so he says

But no I don't I won't I go I'll go back counselling as soon as
she's open I'll go but I have nothing but I don't sleep I'll go to

CIARA

The post office is in the petrol station.

So's the bus stop, the butcher's, the chemist's and the Chinese.

So there's a queue.

People stare at me like I can't stare back. Maybe I'm familiar.
Maybe I look like Nana.

I don't stare back. I keep my head down and double-check the
site map. Looks good.

Behind the counter, a girl is pushing ham through a slicer.

Recorded delivery?

This counter's for fuel she says. Sharon'll sort me.

She shouts at the chemist to come do post office.

But Sharon's doing pharmacy.

She'll be over in a minute she goes, ham piling on her hand.

I browse.

Radio's playing news. Farmers' national protesting. Oh right, the tractor.

Ham-girl goes round the back a minute, comes back shouting number forty-four prawn crackers.

Sharon calls out a name. Ger Slevin.

What a weird /

It's the guy off the bridge.

Saltwater.

I drop my head and look up through my eyebrows.

He stands from his chair then limps to the counter.

Takes his prescription then whispers to Sharon.

Brandy! she goes. And what about his Antabuse?

Fair enough. She doesn't want him dropping dead. Don't serve him Ruth she says.

Anyway Ruth's gone out the back with a post bag. A van speeds off the concourse to the motorway.

Ger's pleading, but Sharon's a no. He shuffles out.

I avoid his eye.

Sharon hangs up her white coat, then comes through to the post office.

I need this next-day delivery. Thinking too I better book my bus.

It'll get there Friday she says.

Today's Wednesday. Tomorrow's Thursday.

Today's post is finished. She points to the van that's already gone.

It'll go tomorrow. Get there Friday.

Plain rice and twenty unleaded! Ruth has some lungs on her.

Friday. Fuck. Friday, like. Sake.

I pay.

*

Outside the garage the smell of petrol the fumes of traffic.

The sky is rosier. Sun blushing through pollution.

All the cars is more what I remember, even though it's new, all plastic and new.

Red-brick ground, moss in the gaps.

Just beyond the road there's the fields towards the river.

The cottage one side; the site the other.

I'm about to phone Mam.

Fuck.

The paperwork arrives Friday. Team Monday. I'm back Tuesday latest.

It'll be fine. We'll work something out. A little delay doesn't mean I'm cancelling.

I even take out my phone to ring. I should tell her.

It's how she takes the news though –

Not sure what happens next.

Hear the footsteps first.

Feel his fingers prodding.

And mumbling asking pleading.

Shout 'leave me alone' but it comes childish like 'leemeelone!'

'Leemelone' like. All the shouting, Sharon runs out. Tells him to piss off and he limps across the fields.

An hour later you're still there drinking sugary tea, embarrassed.

He's harmless she says. A drinker, just, but with a new liver. Just a lonely old man who lives near the river.

You – who?

You – the fuck, like?!

You.*

Okay; *you* don't know what's happened.

How you – went from him asking you softly to get him a naggin to you fucken screaming crying and mortified.

It's embarrassing. It's it's it's. Get a grip. Like you never met an addict or.

Shivering and.

But something in his voice and in his hand, you –

No idea.

*

You call Mam later.

It goes how you think it might. Mostly.

Here's what you'll do, you'll –

BRÍD

(*Interrupting*.) Outside the counsellor's all those questions the door handle's hot

I can't go into it all again I can't go back I go way and walk

My earliest memory and I cry what every day just for thirst I walk away

Garden grass is burning brown young women chest down browning backs trees climbing kids the world is summer it nearly feels good

The sun is good until it's bad the trees are good until you fall and what about thirst no water wave but

How can the world be anyway right when happiness comes from doing what you shouldn't?

---

* Mark this 'I' to 'You' transition clearly.

I want to go forward don't want to go back

Walk Pill Bottle House Salt Baby Save Rain Calm Leave

Close enough I keep it going starting from the end then a voice a little voice have you any children no a littler voice going smile here missus hello

It's me

No I'm here so that's not me

But she's the spit is she

Missus smile she goes

Then louder from behind a wild-looking woman haiy leave the poor old woman sorry sorry

I'm the poor old woman sorry this little girl is from the wild-looking mother

Get it straight what it is a little girl holding a camera look I found I'll take your picture and her mother staggering saying sorry she's no manners and she's as pleased as punch to meet me please and pleased as punch am I

Pretty little thing in a little white dress four or five running down the garden

And is it the heat or the tiredness or the shock of it all I don't know only the next thing I'm sitting in their garden and the mother asking would I have something stronger for the shock

Just for the shock sure just the one just for the shock will I

*

I spend the afternoon with them and it's as nice so nice a child's a joy forever well not forever but as long as they're young I feel worn with joy when I get home

He comes in from work and looking sideways but he says the counsellor went well I say it did

I got talking I tell him to the woman and the girl and it's nice to have a friend he says it's nice to have a friend

He goes to start dinner and sees I'm already cooking

He's delighted me looking so well

Ham in the oven chewing cloves as I go

Pop one in his mouth he laughs

I tell him about my friend he cracks the clove between his teeth
his breath and my breath no hiding

I tell him about the girl how friendly and he cutting his ham
I can see he's sad I say

I'm sorry we never had one

and he says

it could be him that should be sorry and sure

Don't we have each other always

I feel it all feel better feel love I forget why I ever felt wrong
I forget can't I forget be allowed to forget

Isn't there joy in forgetting

But I don't say any more I say I said I'd mind the child some
day right he says I say some business she's sorting knows
nobody local

Well he says if I think I'm up to it but

But he says puts down his fork and knife the second it's too much
the knife and fork scrape the plate please he says I have to tell him

The knife falls sideways out of the tine of the fork and onto the
plate it clatters it falls

The fat pads on his fingers close I hear them press

He says nothing now looking sideways I say it won't get too
much knowing full well though knowing it might but I feel
good at the minute and I want to keep feeling

He knows he says but just in case –

In case of what? In case I can't have a second without a second
thought everything's fine I'm getting better sure amn't I fine

I throw away my dinner without eating any good

Can't I have a drop of joy without being reminded what's
below it

CIARA

(*Dreaming.*)

Sandy beach, laughing. Chips, ice cream.

Then a wave. Growing, huge.

Swimmers scream, surfers get vertigo.

The wave won't break. It comes ashore, keeps growing.

The world carries on underwater.

No one believes there was a time before the wave.

No one's ever heard of a beach.

BRÍD

May's pure craic she's gas

Lost in the sticks and a child and all

Left her husband lost her mother all on her own

Trying to sell but she'll stay if she has to enrol the girl local if
they're here past the summer

And her so smart her books go out and play no the sun is bad
the acid rain

May laughs she knows everything laughs and pours

Likes a drink but has good taste

And look Walk House Bottle whatever no counsellor

Like I feel good don't I I feel good isn't that enough don't
go back

I ask how old her mother was she says I don't want to go into
that we're still here aren't we look forward yes I agree and

Underneath it all is only more of what's beneath

He comes home to find me singing and messing cooking but
I've forgotten to put on the cooker so dinner'll be late

He lies across the couch have we milk he goes we don't I know I'll get it myself at the shop

Outside the night's not cool the sun is bad of course aha

I walk and sure I'm halfway there when I remember the shop's closed by now but I'm halfway back when I do I forget I know I'm out it's nice to be out so I walk I just walk I keep walking and I don't know how long but what harm it's only walking

The night is cool now I feel good maybe I'll sleep

He finds me later hours sitting by the dried-out river calm who is he look at him who is he look at him have you eaten he goes no have you drank no comment who is he crying who am I oh it's him

CIARA

A wave is coming.

BRÍD

We lie that night and me not sleeping him not sleeping

I'm better no sleep than him tossing turns I won't ask him how he is

Later he's up hunting in the kitchen I follow

Holding the cloves he clocks the breath say nothing

He digs deep into the presses finds my brandy

Would he hit me

No he swings away open the back door open and fucks the bottle into the yard

Glass smash pissing little rivers dribble into grass

Smell it from here powerful it'll be dry before morning it's gone

Bastard

CIARA

You wake up heavy. The day is heavy. Your dreams were heavy.

Mouth. Salt lips. Water.

What did you dream? A fight or? Still wrecked.

Could sleep again. Nothing to do till they get the paperwork.

A day at least. What'll you do?

You spoke to Mam; not now.

Laptop, search 'Things to do Dungiven.'

Four results [!]. Two for the bus, one for the beach which is not that close, one for riverside walks.

Search bus times from Dungiven.

Annadarmot.

You had to tell her. That you wouldn't be back. She didn't even know you were gone.

You told her where you were.

It better be worth it. If it turns out to be nothing after all this hassle?

Can see outside the day's well-dawned but duller; headache grey.

Don't want to go out.

It better not rain though; that lake, like that – (*Snap on 'that'*.) Better not.

Search bog bodies Ireland.

Clonycavan, Croghan, Cashel.

Sacrifice. Volunteers. Offerings to nature.

Harvest. Sunshine. Fear.

Can you imagine?

You can imagine frightened people.

Tearing themselves apart as the world heats up.

You can imagine being scared. Of the future. Of the past.

But can you imagine anyone saying: 'Take me'?

'I'll die so you can live in peace.'

'Bury me in bogland and put your fear behind you.'

*

Riverside walks. And what if it rained?

Go see the remains.

Understand the sacrifice.

You burrow out of bed.

The false ache of your dream. Do you nearly remember?

No. It's got you rotten, but it's gone.

*

You got excited talking to Mam.

Saying it looked good. Could be major.

Forgetting it meant a delay.

Telling her it was Annadarmot.

Her saying nothing so you going on, saying you hardly remembered until you saw the post office – remember the Push Pop? – and the ould fella at the petrol station.

You don't tell her you cried or that.

You don't tell her you're drunk either, that you bought yourself the brandy that you wouldn't buy for him.

You never talk to her about drink.

Maybe she can hear it. You go quiet trying to pretend you're sober. But she'd know, wouldn't she?

Then she says:

'You were never in Annadarmot.'

'Nana lived there. But you were never there.'

And then she says can't you come back tomorrow?

They can do without you. She needs you. You promised. Don't let her down.

Come back in the morning can't you?

BRÍD

Morning comes as morning does already hot

Steam rising off the bog he says come on

He marches me up the village past the shop no stopping

Arrive at the counsellor's knocking hard she lets us in

Now Bríd what happened can you say I say nothing

Can we start with some exercises then start where you like

Walk she goes I say nothing House *ciúnas* Pill nah

She says she has a terrible memory too forgets appointments people's faces

It's normal to forget but when you stop remembering what's happening now it can come back when you don't expect

Take her she says when she was small her auntie died in front of her

What

Only small four or five Auntie 'ating toffees and she clowning too like always when she swallows one she makes a face d'y'know and my wan laughs and Auntie coughs and my wan laughs more and Auntie stops her eyes stood out pure quiet and my wan still laughing thinking Auntie's joking even after Mammy comes

And Mammy never said thinking ignorance is best but still and all not a toffee could my wan eat without throwing it up again

So on some level she knew on some level remembered but thought 'twas fine 'twas normal

Normal four or normal five communion dress garden path Dadda digging Mamma roaring don't you dare let Bríd get dirty Dadda doesn't looks away before that though he comforts her while she cries at her own mother's I want to hug but take that child away she goes and before that Mamma trying to hug a hug for Granny and Granny though just pushing her away like don't be pawing and no hug never except at Christmas

Dadda'd drop a drop a' brandy Mammy's tea with cloves and lemon a hug from Dadda and a kiss even Mamma and the dryness of her cheek and the lines near her lips only young but so dry and so hard except the odd drop a' brandy Dadda'd sneak before he'd send me early to bed and only then some laughter in the house

So it's joy at the heart a drink to unlock do I have to remember how unhappy we are

Remember her and Dadda dead no comfort for her young widow no comfort from her dry and silent no joy never no not nearly no way

Walk House Pill Bottle Baby Save Salt Leave Calm Rain

That's very good Bríd she goes

Rain Calm Leave Salt Save Baby Bottle Pill House Walk

Excellent but underneath

No nothing really nothing serious I know I'm no I'm right

She walks me out he says should she go back the clinic the city NO I'll go nowhere I'll run I'll NO I won't

But no she goes she thinks not yet they're very busy and we can manage can't we Bríd?

I'm going nowhere for nobody I say we can of course and so we go

CIARA

The day's cloying at you. The sky's a seal, a lid.

Hawing onto glass. Litres of spent breath, no breeze.

Dew on the rushes now. Spring in the moss.

Standing inside a yawn.

That river there is tidal. An inch above sea level.

An inch!

You're standing at the bottom of an ocean in the future.

The near future.

There's salt in the soil, you can smell it.

You lift the tarp heavy grey to look at the body again.

If it rains and you've not seen his face.

Kneel and get in closer.

His mouth is caked in soil. Just a touch to see.

You brush gently at his cheeks. The dirt falls. The flesh stays.

Brush more.

So small. Delicate features.

'Magine how soft he was, going quietly to his killers.

To save his people. Any hope for you?

Climate protests. Farmers' strikes.

What fed you will eat you alive.

He went so his people could breathe.

Any hope for you?

You were never here / No, you badly want to start.

No halters, bludgeons, cuts.

So how did they do it?

Drowning? A foot pressing down on his head.

You'd need to dig right down to know.

What does she mean never here?

You remember, don't you?

Tch – you musta been. Why else freak out at yerman?

You can feel it even if you can't picture it.

People forget. Doesn't mean –

You were here.

There's a difference between forgetting and never knowing.

There's the rain but no you're crying dropping tears all down your wrists.

It hasn't rained in weeks.

If it did? And you lost it all for nothing?

Saltwater off your face, without a sample?

You need something to show. Something to take back to town, right?

You get your snips, your plastic.

You steady your hand. That brandy.

Lift at a lock, a wiry knot.

The hair, the hair.

Can you untangle?

Pull at it. Nearly.

Pull more, careful.

Soil runnels at the sides. The ground cracks eggshell under.

One more tug and snip then – shit.

It's…

You…

It's… [fucked.]

(*Long beat – she has jeopardised the whole find by digging too soon.*)

No one saw you. No one for miles. Get lost out here forever nearly.

Coulda been like that before. It's loose and muddy but. The digging team won't notice. Once it doesn't rain…

[You'll have to] Delete your photos.

And the snipped hair in your hand. You've done that now, it's done. That's yours.

Maybe it's better to have it? Better to have that much.

If it does rain they'll be grateful.

If it doesn't, makes no odds.

Plus it hasn't rained for weeks, like.

That's the whole be-all and end.

Pull the tarp back into place, peg it down as hard's you can.

The ground is brittler still.

It'll have to do.

Here's what you'll do, you'll write your notes, delete your photos, hide the hair.

The team gets here you'll lead the dig. Hannah'll let you.

You'll excavate and publish; you'll lecture and present.

You'll take a post abroad and buy your own place.

Somewhere high.

You'll get away from renting and Ireland and flood plains.

You'll start with your notes. So you need Pat Whelan's statement.

Stand up. Start walking.

BRÍD

(*On 'walking'*.) me home like a child not a happy one like
a prisoner not a guilty one thinking he'll get it once we're home
I swear to good fuck boy both barrels don't be pawing

But instead don't we see sitting on our back-door step little girl
white dress sitting down not a care

Where's your mother I say she says I've run away

The sun's outrageous her dotey skin why don't we go inside and
drink would you have some milk

I tell him May's address go get her you I'm fine

I ask what happened but she says not a word only shows me her
book and drinks her milk hungrily would she eat? Come with me.

CIARA

You walk, and even as you go you see the sun's fingers prodding
through clouds, shuffling the motorway, glinting off cars.

Left, the back of the cottage. Ya?

You know it like you know it but maybe just from yesterday.

Back door's open. Broken glass winking in the yard.

Do you remember?

Yer man with the limp went down from the garage? There. And
you saw him back on the bridge too, so. (*She's triangulating*.)

The ditch is wide and deep.

A caulk of salt lines the bank. What was high tide.

You can't cross here now.

Leave the cottage on your left she said.

Leave it. Traipse the bog.

BRÍD

Bogs are wetlands made of peat she's reading plants and water
breaking down the plants don't rot they grow in what's that word

Waterlogged

deeper every year so you know how old your buried treasure
measuring how deep

Can we look for treasure Auntie Bríd?

The way she says Auntie fills up my heart.

I'm toasting bread to give her lunch

She won't eat till I eat I eat some it tastes good I eat some more

It fills me up and golden feel I will we look for treasure

Hurray!

We've already found some

She's kicking her feet her bare little feet her shoes off sure
lookit she feels so at home

Clatter plates finished her mother's at the door with him

Thanking me and thanking him saying oh relief

She's had the worst day sorting probate but I can smell the drink
still I realise I've no thirst feel full of bread and golden and she's
oh God her little girl she's fine but she forgot she just forgot

And who are we to say who are we we say go on no hassle
we're delighted any time she's always welcome

We looked for treasure the little one says but May no answer
gripping arm marching her home or holding for balance we're
always here

CIARA

(*On 'here'*.) drinking tea, Pat fills you in on yerman Ger Slevin.

An odd fish. Forever walking. Ruined his legs.

Drinking his post-office pension.

The wife left him years ago, can't blame her, though he's harmless enough.

She was a divil for the drink; a wanderer.

Soft though too, she was, and daft, going missing.

Off she'd go until she came back.

One day I suppose she stopped coming back.

He only took up the drink himself after she was gone.

You eat homemade bread, drink sweet and milky tea. Feel better, maybe. Coming back to yourself.

I. (*Using the first person doesn't take.*) Nearly. But.

You ask Pat did she know Nana.

You can't remember which street. You haven't seen it yet, but you remember a terrace, a tree out the front.

You know that for sure cos you've seen photos.

Why tell her that? Like she heard you talking to Mam.

There's nowhere near like that she says.

They knocked houses for the motorway though, and does she maybe does she think they cut down trees to build the garage?

Do you want more bread and jam?

You don't thanks very much.

She signs the form, you file it.

*

Saplings behind the petrol station.

And on the red-brick concourse, the grates are half-buried, the new road washing over the old.

So it could be:

That the shop's in the garden.

The pumps are the front doors.

And the wall you're standing on is where the kitchen was.

Where you sat eating bread drinking sugary tea.

Or was that at Pat's just now?

Is it here? Does it look like it?

Wouldn't have to dig down far.

That photo you found with your schoolbooks. Framed now on your shelf.

Nana and Mam together. The only one you have.

Nana in the garden. Mam shading her eyes.

Afternoon sun.

So they're facing roughly west.

West. Behind the petrol station.

It could be here.

And were you here?

You can see it – but were you?

You're not in the photo. But remember the angle? (*From below.*)

Blurry; finger on the lens;

A child playing with a camera?

Making them stand beside each other?, your two favourite people, so you could have a go at snapping.

You should show it to Mam. Look like. You took that. Make her admit it.

She won't.

Is this how it always will be? Everything her way.

A woman who can't look after herself right, won't eat if she's eating alone, makes you feel like an idiot, makes you feel about *this* fucken size.

Take the picture.

Mam impatient. Nana fading.

Frowning at the sun and frowning at her daughter.

BRÍD

Don't see them for a while

Concentrate on getting better

Try my best to remember

Not here not yet try my best to get better.

CIARA

You're there a while, trying your best to remember, fucken – (*She strains to remember like it's a physical act.*) when the chemist comes out.

The post-office woman – Sharon – asking if you're okay.

You tell her.

Fuck it.

You tell her you'd swear you've been here before, you think your nana might've lived here, does she remember what was there before the petrol station?

But she's talking about yerman Ger saying she hasn't seen him since the thing yesterday.

Did you call the Guards on him? Cos he doesn't deserve it she says. He's not a well man.

She's asking you what you're up to with Pat Whelan and the bogland.

You haven't called anyone you say.

Saltwater waves.

You're an archaeologist.

You don't know anything about anything.

Behind her looms a shadow.

A shape in the sky.

You can't see it at first with the sun.

Droning. Getting closer.

It's a shark.

A buzzing shark's head, floating straight for you.

You can't take this.

Your heart's washing in your ears.

The heat steals the air from your breath.

Salt. Leave. Calm. What?

Where are you?

Under everything.

Sharon turns and roars at Ruth and bats the shark away.

Ruth comes roaring too, remote in hand, like leave it alone!

She rescues the blimp, checks the camera's alright and sets it off sailing again.

Sharon says don't fly it near the pumps.

If it overheats we'll go up in flames.

Waves of fire.

It's rising higher.

You start to breathe again.

Imagine the shots she's getting. Not just your terror, but the landscape underneath.

The river, the bridge, the site, the cottage.

Ruth's sorry, but you're laughing.

Sorry, you go, that drone thing scared the shit a' you.

You thought you were going mad.

Still laughing.

(CIARA*'s actually laughing now, warmly.*)

Oh man. (*Still as though to Sharon.*) You slept all wrong last night.

Sharon's sorry too, about Ruth and the drone, about Ger, about
not knowing about your nana.

You're sorry about yerman.

If you see him.

Of course, you say, of course.

And the shark drone sails on, a dot over bogland.

Keep looking even when you can't see

BRÍD

We don't see them for a while

I concentrate my exercises

Walk House I have it down

I eat a bit each day eat more

Putting on weight start thinking clearer.

Realise there's nothing under only pain.

My father drank to feel some joy, my mother never drank.

Her mother drank and wasn't kind so my mam was sober till
Dadda died.

I didn't like her drunk but I didn't like her sober her old bones
sore crying out to be touched.

It's not my pain she gave it to me nor was it hers she got it
given it's coming up from all the under.

But I have love he loves me now no children but we have
each other.

If this is what it is why fear it I'm not happy when I'm drinking
I only think I am.

I only think I am.

I want to be here not back in the clinic.

I don't want to hurt hurt him or hurt me.

CIARA

You look until you don't see

Don't look until you see

BRÍD

And soon you see the days get cooler.

I rest the days not sleeping.

I never sleep that can't be true I must forget.

No dreams and underneath it all my memories aren't dangerous they're empty.

I'm fine I will be fine.

He walks me to the counsellor not gripping, we hold hands instead two ould young ones it's gas.

I'm doing well she says, I am.

Ger's looking after me, he is.

We pass the house the garden the tree but no sign mother nor daughter I'm sorry we'd no goodbye.

I could leave it all from here.

See out myself like this at rest I could. If nothing more happened, I'd see

It's not my pain it was passed to me.

It's not my pain it was passed to me.

The heat recedes I still don't sleep,

It's not my pain it was passed to me see –

CIARA

    Petrol station.
    Motorway.
    Bogland.

(*To the right.*)   B&B.
                                                                  Village.
                                                              Post office.

(*To the left.*)   Pat Whelan's
                              The bridge.
                              The site.

(*Between them, she goes.*)   The river.
                                         The ditch.
                                         The cottage.

(*Over the course of this next she goes from laughing at herself
to streaming tears, maybe trying to laugh at herself by the end,
but not, just crying without acknowledging it.*)

You're tramping now across the bog, still laughing.

The dread you felt – the way you gave in to it.

When all it was was a balloon on a camera.

Maybe your feelings are just your feelings and the world has
nothing to do with it.

Maybe the dread you feel is the same dread as always.

You had it as a kid, then Dad left, so you thought you were
psychic.

You had it graduating into recession when the world went broke
and crazy.

You have it now and you think it's cos the sun's been shining
months and it shouldn't be it really shouldn't.

But you don't miss your dad, and the dread's still there.

And they say the recession's over but the dread's still there.

And maybe sometimes the sun just shines. Maybe it's not
always catastrophe.

Or maybe it is but it's nothing to do with this feeling.

Cos I'm talking to you now, like I'm a person who understands
anything, and I don't, not a thing, I don't even know as I reach
the cottage push the back door open whether I was ever in this

hallway or if I just need to think I was to explain breaking in, to explain to myself why I feel this pain to finally explain this pain I've been feeling forever though it's not my pain it was passed to me I've gone into it but it isn't mine I'm gone in under I'm altogether gone

BRÍD

WHAT AM I MEANT TO DO WITH YOU

Hear it from the field. A sharp and knives-out shouting ringing someone's in our house.

ANYTHING COULDA HAPPENED

Me and Ger together evening pick him up from work post office home across the fields but see no hear the roar

WHAT AM I MEANT TO DO

Someone's in our house

DRIVE ME FUCKEN DEMENTED

Someone reach the window rushing fumbling back door open someone's in our house

It's May the mother but she's shouting screaming roaring at poor Ciara little child

YOU LITTLE LITTLE LITTLE LITTLE WHAT AM I HOW CAN I COPE

Rush the kitchen c'mon c'mon stop that now but no no heed she's

RUNNING OFF LIKE THAT – LOOK WHAT HAPPENS

Raining tablets down her throat and the child in tears

SERVE YOU RIGHT IF I DIE she goes

Slugging brandy smell it sweet

Poor baby crying, call her, Ciara!

Ger is calling come here come here he whisks her safe up in his arms. She's crying screaming 'Leemelone!' 'Mammy! Mammy! Leemelone!'

May stares she doesn't remember can't tell like where or who

Ger has the child hands her to me.

Take Ciara away, get out, he tells me, course I say, I take her.

I hug her close, poor little. Can't see for all the tears.

The two of us together. The two of us leave.

I say as I go, Ger, the paracetamol.

The tablets Ger for God's sake look the pills the bottle paracet–

See him jump and pour the salt hot water glass the tears down Ciara poor baby's face

And May he makes her drink it up saltwater save her throw it up

Let's go we go I grab the keys soothing leaving head post-office shop

Clock the bottle leaving no just bring the child to safety

The clouds are rumbling but no rain still

Just the two of us together the two of us alone.

*

We sit alone post-office shop. I've let her eat whatever. She's jabbering away 'ating lollies acting like she's already forgotten. Misses me phoning the ambulance. Misses the blue lights on Main Street.

A woman comes official like and takes the child away

It's time to go poor baby's gone goodbye she waves and eats her pop

We'll never see each other again

Watch her leave like have to leave then go back to the house

CIARA

And the feeling's there.

That this is familiar.

Cleaner now, even if it's older.

Paint over what used to be paper.

Sun-bleach over what used to be, what?

A row of shoes?

Shoes-off even with the drinking.

Scratch of carpet on little bare feet.

Avoid the kitchen. Definitely. No question.

Living-room door's ajar.

And in the neatness still surprising, he's lying on the couch.

Shallow breaths. Sleeping calm.

Same clothes as yesterday.

His Antabuse is open, two tablets gone, no more.

The prescribed dose. This is not a tragic scene.

A bucket beside him. Side effects are no joke.

But brandy too. Just out of reach.

He bought a bottle somewhere.

Seal's not broken yet.

It's a nightmare drinking on those tablets. That's how they work.
So drinking feels worse than drying.

The brandy is the fear of detox. Case getting better feels worse
than getting worse.

BRÍD

The silence shrill no noise around the knives are out alone.

Ger's not back maybe making statements. It's growing cold,
I clean.

Eight of sixteen tablets gone. Only half the brandy.

Half the bottle sitting there, half's a lot.

They'll pump her stomach to be safe tide out.

It won't be nice. She might survive. The girl she'll get her back.

Go out get out while all is calm sure now's the chance just go.

Take the bottle he won't drink it take it go and leave

CIARA

Make one noise and he'll waken.

He could lift the lid on everything.

'Do you know what happened here?'

'Do you know what this feeling is?'

Could bring everything to light.

More like he'd wonder who the fuck's standing over him.

Will he think he's dead? That someone's here to finish him off?

Look at him.

He does seem nice.

That feeling yesterday.

Whatever it is.

It isn't him.

Sharks in the sky come in waves never breaking.

Best thing clear out.

He'll feel better once he's slept.

Take away the brandy while he's sleeping just go.

It's a practised manoeuvre.

He won't ever know who.

You were never even here.

BRÍD

It's dark tonight and starless heavy. Been a long time since it rained but it will rain I think tonight

I cross the field beneath the clouds.

(*Pause*.)

I drink.

(*Pause*.)

I cross the ditch the little plank bridge

The dried-out lake

Search for treasure

I'm exhausted so I sit

The brandy's warm it warms me through

Our pain is not just ours alone it got given up from down below.

Could it stop here? With me, it could sure

But who am I?

Too tired to start and end all that

The rain falls and fills the world around me and I start to nod beneath it

Laughing nearly to feel it thunder falling sweetly on my body

Runnels down my head like what's in there?

No rush to go anywhere water rushing round me who

Could fall asleep here finally so I could

So I do

CIARA

This wave of calm washes over when you click the door
behind you.

This feeling of fucken benevolence.

Sweeps over me so completely.

I hardly notice my relief that it's raining.

I nearly laugh.

And then I remember.

My body in the lake.

*

I rush across the bog trying to find a spot to cross

And there a plank a wedge a bridge I tightrope nearly fall
but don't.

The site is close but first I see the tarpaulin sailing past me.

The turlough's filling up.

The body loose in its place.

I kneel in down beside.

The water rises round my thighs.

I want so much to turn it. Look it in the face and see.

Don't let it wash away completely.

All I can do is rebury.

Try packing mud around the body.

It turns to slop in my hand.

Try and raise a mound around it.

It all washes away.

It's all washing away.

I try and bury down before it all gets lost and washes.

I try and there I am I'm trying and the rain just falls and fills.

*

I fall asleep and stay asleep throughout the night without one dream.

I wake up late and it's still lashing but it sounds so good I stay in bed.

I even feel alright maybe, even if the site is fucked.

Still, I put off emailing Hannah till my bags are packed and I check the buses.

Any bus going anywhere. She gets back straight away.

She can't believe it's gone. The turlough I explain.

I don't hear back at first. I'm thinking, shoulda never touched it. It kept so long before me.

Finally, a reply. Any pics?

No; I forgot. Her: Right.

I have to send my notes and she'll see what happens next. If there's hassle I'll have to answer. But a lake is a lake. Anything coulda happened.

(*Phone rings. Cancels the call.*)

Meanwhile there's a ringfort over near the coast.

Can I head there please, if I don't have to come straight back?

She's annoyed alright. But she's not firing me.

(*Phone rings. Cancels the call.*)

I don't have to come straight back.

*

I'm huddling in a shelter near the garage. The bus is due.

The fluorescent light inside the shop. A beacon.

Ruth's selling milk to Ger. Sharon's gossiping with Pat.

They can't see me here inside the rain.

The sky's a grey seal, a lid, a wall of water.

(*Phone rings. Maybe leaves it but doesn't answer. Maybe puts it in her pocket and lets it ring.*)

Wheels slosh hiss across badly draining motorway. They'll need to rebuild or watch it wash away.

It rains in strings, seaweed, hair, wisping down across the bog.

It looks out there like it's been raining forever.

Like if the sun had ever shone, the sky's already forgotten.

A Nick Hern Book

Flights and *Sink* first published in Great Britain in 2020 as a paperback original by Nick Hern Books Limited, The Glasshouse, 49a Goldhawk Road, London W12 8QP, in association with One Duck

Cover designed by Martha Hegarty

Designed and typeset by Nick Hern Books, London
Printed in the UK by Mimeo Ltd, Huntingdon, Cambridgeshire PE29 6XX

A CIP catalogue record for this book is available from the British Library

ISBN 978 1 84842 939 0

www.nickhernbooks.co.uk

 facebook.com/nickhernbooks

 twitter.com/nickhernbooks